So Long Europe, Hello South Africa

Tall Tales and Adventures
By
Herman Thorbecke

A Memoir or Maybe Not...

Available in print and digital eBook format.

Published by Zephyr Publishing Inc.
www.zephyrpublishing.com

This edition published in 2011

www.hermanthorbecke.com

I dedicate this book to the memory of my
son Bert and daughter Martine

Bert, Martine and Rudy
No need for shoes

Acknowledgements

This little book would not have come to completion without the undying encouragement and support of a great team of people. First of all there is my wife, Lea, who patiently suffered my irritable behavior during the many periods of writers block and then stoically sat through my readings of every new bit of text I managed to come up with.

The editing efforts and constructive comments of the core members of the Clarkesville Writing Society were essential to the completion of the manuscript. So were Ronen Madjar's computer skills and infinite patience in formatting the manuscript for Microsoft Word.

Before this book saw the light of day, I already had two fans. They are my lovely niece Hanna Staartjes in Holland and equally lovely, very good South African friend, Clarabelle van Niekerk, now living in Pennsylvania and herself an accomplished author and illustrator. Both always cheered me on with their helpful criticism and assurances that my stories were worthy of publication. Thanks also to my dear son, Rudy Thorbecke, for sorting through a stack of old pictures in his collection and providing me with usable copies, some of which are reproduced in this book.

A number of the pictures, you will find in these pages, were taken by Nancy and Joseph Gill. They courteously agreed to let me use them. Please visit the website of these generous globetrotters at **www.worldglobetrotters.com**, where you will find the originals in glorious color. You will not be disappointed. Their work clearly illustrates how much has changed in respect of race relations since the years I spent in beautiful South Africa.

Many thanks to Steve Goulet at Zephyr Publishing for getting my book ready for the printed page.

And finally there are my two Standard Poodles, Leeuw and Chester who steadfastly flanked me while I was seated all those many hours in front of my computer. Although, some may argue that they were just waiting for me to take them for another walk, I firmly believe they were intent on mingling their own creative impulses with mine. OK, don't say it please. Don't even think it. No, this book is no doggerel!

Contents

Introduction

The stories in this little book are just that — stories about my experiences as I remember them, growing up in The Netherlands and later living in South Africa. Most of these tales deal with my life and that of my family in South Africa.

I have included the pre-Africa chapters to stress and define the rather bewildering and chaotic circumstances of my youth. With the war years and the relaxed attitude of my parents in respect to my upbringing, there was little structure to my life until I married — too early — and migrated away from my origins in order to find a different world. At the time I emigrated to South Africa I was young, very young and also rather impulsive and irresponsible. Always looking for greener grass and no matter how high the fence, I would manage to get to the other side. Variation was very much the spice of my life.

My family will almost certainly not remember some of these experiences, either because they did not share them or simply, because some of these things happened the way I like to remember them. Since the African adventures are partly overlapping, they are not always presented in chronological order.

The names and characters of people featured in these stories, other than my immediate family members, have been changed to protect their privacy. For that same reason some of the incidents and the places they occurred in, have been altered and fictionalized. Any resemblance to actual persons, living or dead, events or locales is therefore coincidental.

Moreover, if I represent myself in these stories mostly as a decent sort of a fellow, some may want to disagree, and as to the events described, others will most likely dispute their veracity. Keep in mind that they were written to amuse and entertain. To that effect, I may on occasion have embellished the facts a little. Call it artistic license.

Cornelia, September 19, 2011.

Chapter 1

END OF THE WAR

Before the end of the war I had a very scary encounter with a German soldier. It was terrifying and for a moment, I thought I was going to die. On my way home from school, I had marked the greatcoat of the German with orange colored chalk. This was a game my friends and I had played before. That day I used orange chalk in celebration of Queen Wilhelmina's birthday. Orange, as that is the color of the Dutch Royal Family.

It was August 31, 1944 and after making my mark, I then ten years old, thin and scrawny, and dressed in hand-me-downs, ran as fast as I could. However, this time that was not fast enough. On previous occasions, I had always been able to outrun the soldiers with ease and getting caught had not been one of the rules of this game. I must have picked on a real athlete. The German was after me, his hob-nailed boots hammering loudly on the pavement, coming ever closer. I tried to evade my pursuer as well as I could but was no match for this hulking brute. When he caught up with me, he tripped me and I fell flat on my face.

I knew I was done for. It was common knowledge that Germans showed no mercy. I made a last attempt to get away, kicking out at him as hard as I could, but the soldier was too quick for me. Sidestepping my kicks he grabbed me by the collar of my jacket, drew me to my feet, and said in a mixture of German and Dutch, "You are a very stupid little boy, but you are also very lucky. Lucky, that you did this to me and not to "Wachtmeister" Kluge. He would have arrested your pappy and then have him shot—for not teaching you to respect the German uniform."

While telling me this, this soldier with his blond hair and steel-grey eyes—this prime specimen of Hitler's Aryan Race—looked very angry, but at the same time took great pains at dusting off my jacket. He then handed me a slab of chocolate and told me, "Now go home to your mammy and never do dim-witted and dangerous things like that again!"

As soon as he released me I ran and ran and ran some more. I came home totally exhausted and my mother, noticing something must have happened, asked why I had been running and why my jacket was all dirty. I was of course not about to tell her what had really occurred and said, "I just tripped over the curb and I'm fine. Don't worry Mom."

In the meantime, she had taken my jacket and in the process of brushing the dirt off— finishing the job started by the German—she found the slab of chocolate. Real chocolate, as this was, we had not seen for years. By that stage of the war, food had become so scarce that we were down to eating sugar-beet soup and flower bulbs.

"Where did you get this or rather, where did you steal this?" She asked.

"I did not steal it. Someone gave it to me. I didn't even ask for it," I answered truthfully.

She naturally did not believe a word of that. During those days of utter deprivation, nobody in his right mind just gave a perfectly good slab of chocolate away, unless it was in payment or exchange for some act or favor. She grabbed me by my shoulders and shaking me like a rag-doll demanded, "For the very last time, where did you get this?"

And out came the whole story. I told it backwards though, starting with, "A nice German gave it to me."

"A nice German, a nice German? There are no nice Germans! What are you — a sympathizer now?"

I now need to ask my readers for a little understanding. My mother's rather harsh reaction can be explained, I'm sure, by her motherly feelings of love and concern. Trying to keep her husband and family of five children fed, healthy and safe, had stressed her out to the limits of her endurance. I have to admit though, at that exact moment I wished I was back in the good care of that kind German.

After a while, the whole truth eventually was sort of shaken out of me, like the dust out of a rug. The chocolate was confiscated and I was sent to my room. The only part I ever saw of my chocolate bar was one little section. I swear I would voluntarily have shared it with my brother and sisters, but cannot avouch with certainty that the allotments would have been totally fair and equal.

* * * * * * *

The next time I was sure my life was coming to an end was during the middle of April 1945. The Allies were advancing to our city of Groningen in the north of Holland. Large parts of Holland had been liberated much earlier, but the Germans, for some perverse reasons of their own, had decided to keep Groningen out of the hands of the Allied armies. Now, history has taught us that the allies did not think the west and north of Holland were of strategic importance and simply by-passed it on their way to Berlin.

The forces sent to free us were Canadian. Since that time all Dutch people of my generation love everything Canadian. Their advance started on April 13, with relentless shelling of our little city for several days. It was on the second day of that bombardment that I again believed I was going to die.

While the entire family, including grandparents and some neighbors whose house had suffered a direct artillery hit, were hidden in the cellar, I was seated on the 'throne' on the ground floor of our house, attempting to do a little bombing of my own. The results of that had been meager until we received a direct hit. I confess that whatever wiping I managed to do was incidental. I clearly remember that a smoking-hot, two inch fragment of the shell that hit our roof, three floors above, had landed on the marble bathroom tiles, missing me by a foot. It gouged out a nice chunk of marble and had it struck me I might not be here to tell the tale.

I reached the cellar in record time, to be received by my very worried mother, who naturally demanded to know where I had been. I received another thorough shaking and was wondering, if I might be safer upstairs.

Fortunately, the Canadians did not use incendiary grenades and my father and grandfather could put out the small fire that this one had started in the attic. Apart from a big hole in the roof, thirty-two broken windows and lots of little holes in the various ceilings, caused by the shell's shrapnel, the damage was not too bad. I remember my dad saying to my mother, "The shock-wave broke the windows — I should have left them open. Very stupid of me!"

Groningen after liberation from the Germans
(It was worth it)

We all remained hunkered down in the cellar. The shelling gradually stopped as the Canadians entered the city. We heard machine-gun and small arms fire all around us, and while this was going on our old-fashioned pull-chain doorbell started to ring frantically.

The men, and that did include me as I sneaked up behind my father and granddad, went upstairs to see who wanted entry. Dad cautiously opened the door and was confronted by two German soldiers who demanded bicycles.

"Haben Sie ein Fahrrad?" and then in case we did not understand German, "Haben Sie fiets?".

My dad told them we had one but that it was useless, as it had no tires. Not only food was scarce, but also everything else. Rubber was in very short supply and our bicycles had been without tires for some time.

The soldier assured my dad that the lack of tires was no problem, but did he have any Schnapps. Here I was shown a somewhat tougher side of my usually very gentle father.

He told them in German, "No Schnapps and now you two get on the bike and go home to Germany, where you belong."

These two guys, apparently used to taking orders, did as they were told and soon were loudly rattling down the cobble stone road on my mother's old bike, one of them on the baby seat. Two, not so impressive members of the German *Master Race*, running for their lives. Who could blame them? We certainly did not.

That same day, several hours after our German visitors had left, the door bell rang again. This time really loud and with apparent urgency. Again, my dad opened the door but now our liberators had arrived. Two young Canadians with blackened faces and camouflage branches stuck in the netting on their helmets. Later I often wondered how much good that did them in a house-to-house fight, in the middle of a city?

They greeted us with, "Have you any whiskey?"

The speaker was somewhat inebriated, his partner fall-on-your-face drunk. In fact, that is exactly what he did right then.

To my utter surprise, my dad calmly told them that

they were welcome to enter, but that they needed to leave their weapons outside. They both carried Sten guns and had a number of hand grenades hanging from their belts. He also told them that there was no liquor in the house other than a bottle of Lemon Gin, which he assured them, would make them sick. He said, "I am a doctor and alcohol is very bad for your health, particularly for your friend here. Come in and rest a little until he has sobered up and then you can go and continue to fight the war."

The not-so-drunk soldier said, "The war is over, all the Germans kaput."

Although his words were tellingly disputed by a loud burst of machine-gun fire down the block, it did seem that the fighting was practically done. Things quieted down and soon we heard people talking in the street. Our two guests had come in and sat around our hallway for a while, handing out chewing gum to all the kids. They seemed to have their pockets full of the stuff. A good thing too, as there were nine of us—five from my family and four from the neighbors.

After they had left and the fighting was definitely over, we all went into the streets where the celebrations were already in progress. People were singing the national anthem and waving the Dutch flag, a flag that we had not seen in the open for all those years of occupation.

We walked along and after a while came upon a scene, I will always remember. Several German soldiers had surrendered. They were guarded by a small detachment of Canadians who after they had told their enemies to empty their pockets, were going through their possessions. One of the Germans had a bloody bandage around his head. He

7

seemed somewhat familiar and as I came a little closer, this soldier looked me over and said in Dutch that had improved somewhat since our previous meeting, "Well, young man have you behaved yourself since we last met or are you still getting into trouble?"

It was my chocolate bar German, of course. I felt a little sorry for him and asked him if he needed any help. I also told the Canadians that this German was a good one, upon which the Canadian sergeant commented, "Son, the only good Germans I know are dead Germans."

The chocolate-bar German actually laughed openly at that and told me, "Don't worry about me. For me the war is over at last and now I can go home to my son."

Chapter 2

FATTENING UP IN DENMARK

The years after the war were meager ones, especially 1945 and '46. Most foods remained rationed, and many of the children really needed more in order to regain their strength and secure normal and healthy development.

Not all European countries had suffered as much from the German onslaught as some, and Denmark with its relatively small population had fared a little better than Holland. Food production in Denmark was almost uninterrupted, and our good northern neighbors offered to help by hosting a large number of Dutch children for a period of six months.

To be eligible, children had to be in a very undernourished condition, and although I never really considered myself to fall into that group, the medical examiner was of the opinion that I and my younger brother and two-year older sister did. I do remember that my father was actually opposed to the whole idea. He believed that many other children needed it more. However, he was firmly overruled by my mother who, I think, wanted a vacation from her three younger brats. Had inclusion of my two other sisters

9

not been ruled out because of their age, I have a feeling we might all have been shipped off to Denmark.

My sister, brother and I were all going to the same village—Hedensted on the peninsula of Jutland. We would each be living with a different family, and although that did seem a little hard on the three of us, it proved to be a workable arrangement as they all lived fairly close to each other. My brother, Martijn and sister, Niza, were across the road from each other and I was to live on a farm about a mile out of the village.

To me the whole thing was just a great adventure, and as I was never much bothered by homesickness I keenly looked forward to the trip. To my mind, six months of not having to go to school was hard to beat. We were duly loaded on the train with some two hundred other children and off we went. It was September of 1945. We were among the 30,000 Dutch children that were sent to England, Switzerland and Scandinavia.

I will always remember that very long train ride. Railway traffic was still disrupted, and since we had to travel through Germany, it took endless stops and starts before we arrived at Bremen, the first major city we traveled through in that country. There was not much left of Bremen. Our hometown had suffered some serious damage at the time the Canadians chased out the Germans, but nothing compared to this. There were very few houses standing and also those, showed plenty of damage. It was therefore even more shocking to see Hamburg, the next big city we came to. In the parts we traveled through there were no buildings upright— absolutely none. All we saw were piles of rubble along streets that had been cleared. There were few people and most of them seemed to have gathered at the train station. Many of them were children, all begging for food. We gave them what we had and I remember asking one of our minders why these poor children could not go to Denmark. They certainly needed it more than we did.

Eventually we arrived in Vejle, the closest city to our destination. There, Mr. Soerenson, my sister's caregiver and foster-father during our stay, awaited us. He was a nice man and immediately managed to put us at ease. We took the ride to Hedensted in Mr. Soerenson's old T-Ford and we arrived there all too soon, as I had not sat in a car for as long as I could remember.

My foster-parents were Mr. and Mrs. Zachariassen, he stern and unfriendly, she loving and kind. I am sure it was not his idea to foster a strange kid from Holland. We had arrived just about at dinnertime and after they showed me my beautiful room, a room much nicer than I had at home, I was told to come down for the evening meal. All this by means of gestures accompanied by a lot of Danish words, none of which I could understand. The meal consisted of home-baked bread, butter, cheese, sliced ham, various jams and honey. A spread of this nature I had not seen for many years.

Mr. Zachariassen and I never managed to get on very well, and the discord started right there during our first meal, a meal that was to begin to fatten me up. His wife packed my plate with buttered bread, a couple slices of ham and a chunk of cheese. I loved cheese, Dutch cheese, but had not yet developed the fine palate, I am now proud to own. To me, the beautiful piece of Fontina on my dish stank to high heaven. I

11

just could not eat it. It actually made me want to puke. Right there and then ended all possibilities of any understanding between Mr. Zachariassen and me. He just could not believe that he was fostering a hungry Dutch kid, a kid that refused to eat the best cheese Denmark had to offer. He was fuming, and I am sure told his wife he had been right the whole time and that these Dutch kids didn't really need the help Denmark was offering. Had it not been for his wife's interference, he would most likely have stuffed the Fontina down my throat.

Things never got better between my "foster-father" and me and certainly not after I released his dog that had been permanently chained to its doghouse. The dog was a nasty piece of work that went into screaming rages at anyone approaching. Some sort of German Sheppard by the name of Hitler. Nice sense of humor had Mr. Zachariassen. After a couple of weeks in Denmark I started to understand and speak the language, and although I had been told that the dog was dangerous and that he would tear me apart if I came too close, I soon made a friend of him by throwing him pieces of Fontina. After a couple of weeks he stopped barking and started wagging when I came close.

As Mr. Zachariassen could only come close to his dog with a whip in his hand, he did not like my palsy relationship to his dog. He took his anger out on the animal by whipping the crap out of him. After another one of those beatings, I released Hitler and he never returned. He must have been smarter than his namesake. My "foster-dad" suspected me, but as I had released the dog without any witnesses, he could never prove my guilt. From there on our relationship went downhill. I did not really mind as I felt that his wife was mostly on my side.

The 1945-46 winter was very severe all over Europe and boy, did I enjoy the ice and snow. I did my first bit of skiing in Denmark. Not that there are any mountains in those parts, but there are some gentle hills and dales, just the thing for beginners like me that had to strap their skis under their everyday shoes—the only shoes I had. It was all a little primitive, but fun. Then there was the big pond, fed by a small creek about a mile from the house, where we went skating. We, included some neighbor children and on occasion my little brother and big sister. Skating on that pond brought me close to my maker for the third time in a matter of two years. This time really close.

We had of course been warned to stay off the ice until it was safe, but who would be the judge of that? As this pond was not far from where my sister lived, I asked her to come along one nice Sunday morning. While everyone was in church—from which we were excused for reasons of our different belief—we strapped on our skates. There were areas on the pond without snow where the skating was best. Unfortunately, those were also the areas where the flow of the river had most of its effect, resulting in thin ice—ice too thin to carry me. Coming across a bad patch at a good pace, I went through and under.

Have you ever been caught underneath the ice? Well, better make sure you never will. I was a good swimmer, but with ice over my head, that ability was of limited use. More important is good luck. On that occasion, I had plenty. My panicky striking out with hands and feet led me back to the nice big hole I had made going in. I could breathe again, but getting out of the very cold water was a different matter. The ice just kept breaking off. My sister had come to the rescue by lying flat on the ice, distributing her weight over the largest possible area. Every time I came closer, she had to retreat as the ice was cracking all around her. Finally, after I thought I was never going to make it out, the ice firmed up. I grabbed my sister's hand, and she managed to pull me out of that freezer only to land into another. The wind had come up and it was cold—too cold for a soaking wet and underfed little boy to stay out there for long. We discarded our skates and ran to the Soerenson home, where the young maid undressed me and rubbed me dry in front of an open fire. She kept rubbing and rubbing until she noticed something that surprised me as much as it did her. She slapped me really hard on my butt and told me to get dressed. What did I do wrong?

By the time we were sent back to Holland after about six months, all three of us spoke Danish as well as we did Dutch. In fact, my little brother's "Dansk" was a lot better than his Dutch. We really did well in that country and all put some serious flesh on our bones. And speaking about food, the highlight of our stay was the Christmas celebration in Denmark. If you think that what you eat sometimes for breakfast is "Danish" you need to visit Denmark at Yuletide.

"Thank you Denmark, for having taken such good care of us. Jeg elsker dig!"

Back to school after Denmark

Herman Thorbecke

Chapter 3

HOOLIGANS 1948 STYLE

I must have been about thirteen years old when I figured out a way to open what was assumed to be a sealed-off doorway leading from our home into an adjacent storage facility, owned by a Coffee, Tea and Tobacco Company. Our home during those years was the same as the one that received a direct hit as described in the first chapter. We lived in Groningen in the most Northern Province of the Netherlands.

I was born in that house and lived there for many years. It was an old four-story structure, of which we occupied the two bottom floors. Although my father was an MD and we as kids considered ourselves to be very privileged, my parents could not afford to buy their own home. Our family home was rented from the Coffee, Tea and Tobacco Company. I remember how on occasion I was sent on the errand of paying the rent at the company head office, down the street.

You will wonder why an MD could not afford to buy a house. Nowadays, doctors live in mansions and spend their weekends and summers in their beach condos or mountain homes. My father believed that charging for medical services was unethical and that it was the duty of the community to provide healthcare to all its members. It was therefore his choice to work as a salaried physician for the City of Groningen, where the poor were treated for free. His offices were located in a rather dingy building owned by the city. Here, with the assistance of one nurse, he "cured" all comers. What's more, he also did house calls on his bicycle! I know that is hard to believe—when did you last receive a house call from your general practitioner riding his bicycle?

However, my father was a blessed man. His patients loved him and rewarded him with whatever tokens of appreciation they could afford, from home baked cakes to freshly butchered rabbits. Let me assure you that during the war years and the first years after the German capitulation, additional food was always welcome.

However, I need to get back to the "secret doorway" into the warehouse. Before I do so, let me describe the house a little. It was located on one of the concentric canals ringing the city. The façade was patrician with a rather grand entry door, at least four feet wide and painted bright red. Four granite steps led to the door, next to which there was a brass pull for the doorbell. When pulled, it caused a large, brightly polished bell inside the house to go berserk. It could be heard into the farthest reaches of this rather large house and beyond. On entering, you walked into a small hallway that led to a long, eight-foot wide passage that ran the full length of the house (some ninety feet). It was tiled in marble, with doors leading from either side into various rooms, the kitchen and servants quarters. Sounds rather grand, but it wasn't really. The entire family parked their bicycles in this marble clad passage and there was a rigid pecking order, determining where one could park. With my three older sisters and parents claiming the best spots, closest to the entry door, I was forced to park all the way at the end. My little brother was really out of luck.

This long passage led to a door going out into a nice, large yard that could have been a beautiful garden if anyone in the family had had an interest in gardening. The makings were there, but during the war, to augment our rations, my mother kept a couple of goats and a dozen or so chickens in that garden and it had just gone downhill ever since. The main attraction of the garden was located on the other side of a wooden fence, separating ours from the neighbor's yard. There, the most delicious apples and pears could be had for the small risk of being caught by the owner of these offerings. He was the stern and seemingly unforgiving father of my friend Bernhard. On one memorable occasion, the old man did catch me and rewarded me with a pretty good beating and a basket of fruit. I did not appreciate that type of generosity and decided to be more careful in the future.

One of the doors in the passage opened to a staircase to the second floor. Halfway up there was a landing and off that another doorway leading up eight steps to end into the sealed door to the warehouse. The door was solid wood and hermetically sealed. There was no doorknob but it did have a keyhole sans key. The secrets behind that door had to be disclosed. You may well wonder what took me so long to figure out how to open that door. I needed a key and asking around at school I found out that one of my schoolmates' father was a locksmith. Paul did not really fit into our little group of mischief-makers, but he would do if he could help us

19

open the door. And that he could. He brought an enormous bundle of keys and assured us that one of them would fit.

He was right. One of the last keys tried turned the lock and with an inviting click the latch slid back. The door opened out but only a couple of inches—not enough to squeeze through. Some heavy object obstructed it. A pleasant tobacco aroma wafted through the partly opened door. Did we already smoke at that age? Of course, and that was one of the reasons for trying to get in there. This company was the maker of Roxy cigarettes, which happened to be my favorite brand.

We pushed and shoved and gradually the door creaked open far enough for Bernard, who was the smallest, to squeeze through and soon the three of us were inside. As it was evening and my parents were out playing bridge, as so often was the case, we did not worry about being detected. I could depend on my sisters to mostly mind their own business.

Now, at our leisure, with the lights turned on we proceeded to investigate. This part of the warehouse appeared to be reserved for product that had been rejected for some reason or another. There were boxes of various brands of smokes and shag tobacco all over the place, including Roxys. From now on, I would be able to keep myself in cigarettes without having to waste my pocket money. Perhaps sell a little on the side?

On the downstairs floor of that part of the building, the company parked three or four cars used by the salesmen. "Look at this; they left the keys in the cars. Let's go for a ride!" announced Paul.

There were two Skodas and one Panhard. You may not

be familiar with these brands of cars. Skodas were quite popular shortly after the war and are still manufactured in Czechoslovakia and available all over Europe. The Panhard was a French car and at one time during the fifties, very successful in the races at Le Mans. It had a two-cylinder engine of only 800 cc that produced 60 hp in a car that weighed about 1500 pounds. Peppy little thing that was. Although I was not into cars at thirteen, I sure was keen to try. I had driven a tractor during the summer vacation on a farm and knew how to operate a clutch. No automatics in those days. I got into the Skoda and drove it around the warehouse a little before deciding that it was time to take it on the road.

The warehouse doors, bolted from the inside, were soon opened wide and the three of us piled in for a little joyride. Initially we had planned to just go round the block, but Bernard wanted to show off our car to his cousins who lived a couple of blocks away. Unfortunately, I was not terribly familiar with the traffic rules. I might have gotten away with it as there was hardly any traffic. However, I did overlook that some of the streets were very narrow and therefore one-way only. Of course, I had to drive up one of those in the wrong direction just at the moment when a policeman on his bicycle came riding along and, needless to say, in the right direction.

Well, what do you do in a case like that? You try to reverse yourself out of trouble only to get in even deeper. I was by then pretty good at going forward, but reversing was not yet among my stronger points and a darned VW, parked along the side of the street, got in my way. We had a lot of explaining to do, most of it to no avail. I was saddled with most of the blame and rightly so. My freedom was severely restricted for a very long time with all manner of rules and regulations aimed at improving my behavior and education. Worst of all, the secret doorway was securely nailed shut and I had to go back to buying my smokes.

The author in his "driving outfit"

Chapter 4

INNOCENCE LOST IN NORWAY

I was sixteen years old when I decided to revisit Denmark, together with Frits, my best high school friend. We were going to hitchhike and the basic plan was to find work on a farm in Denmark, save a little money and then roam around and have a good time in Copenhagen.

We did not inform or consult our parents about the details of our plans. I just told mine we were planning a trip and would be traveling around a little. My mother's reaction was an absent-minded, "No problem, have fun. Just get in touch when you need something and don't stay away too long."

"Don't worry Mom, I'll send you a post card now and then."During the almost ten weeks we stayed away, I never quite found the time to do that. We packed up and left the next day, taking the basics in back-packs—one change of clothes, Speedos, as we were both avid swimmers, sleeping bags, a small cooking pot, metal mugs and some utensils. Our very first lift took us to the border with Germany. We walked across, had our passports stamped and headed for the autobahn—direction Hamburg. We were soon picked up by an older couple in a nice Mercedes Benz on their way to that city. Our high school German was good enough to keep up a basic conversation. To make them feel good, I told them a cock and bull story about always having liked the Germans. The guy was an old military type with some form of nervous disorder that seemed to prevent him from keeping his foot steadily on the gas. The result was a continuous and rather nauseating fluctuation in our speed. I told him I was eighteen years old and that I would not mind helping him with the driving. In Europe you cannot obtain a license before your eighteenth birthday. To my utter amazement, he agreed to have me do the driving. Didn't even ask to see my *license*!

My driving experience could only be described as very elementary and when he stopped the car, got out and invited me behind the wheel, I was asking myself why I had to open my big mouth. In for a penny, in for a pound. I got behind the wheel and with a little initial grinding of the gears got the Merc to move along the autobahn at a steady sixty miles an hour. No problem, everybody happy except Frits, who had to sit in the back with the "General," who according to him not only had a nervous disorder, but a digestive one to boot.

On arrival in the big city of Hamburg, my driving abilities were severely put to the test. I was of the opinion that I passed that test with flying colors, but it was a good thing that even six years after the war, the traffic in Germany was still limited. While driving along Mrs. General had inquired about our plans for the evening and as we had none, she invited us to spend the night at their brand-new beautiful home. Once there, she spoiled us as only a loving Mother would, and later in the evening told us that she had lost her two sons during the Battle of Stalingrad. She assured us that we would always be welcome at their home in Hamburg.

The next morning, after a fabulous breakfast of pancakes, eggs and sausages, we were on our way again, direction Denmark. In those days, hitchhiking was not yet considered a hazard to either the giver or the taker of the lift. We never had to stand too long on the side of the road to find someone willing to take us. As long as there was traffic, we kept moving. Just outside Hamburg, a truck driver on his way to Copenhagen picked us up. Not as nice as a Mercedes perhaps but a perfect match all the same, as we were on our way to a farm on the Island of Sjaelland, the island on which Copenhagen is located. I had heard from friends in Denmark that this very large farm was always short of labor during the summer months. We were dropped off at Roskilde and soon found a ride to the farm that became our home for the next two weeks.

It did not take us long to figure out why this landowner was always short of labor. They worked us for ten to twelve hours a day after a breakfast of oatmeal porridge and a small sausage. At lunchtime we were allowed thirty minutes to eat a lunch that was delivered in the field, usually arriving cold and totally unappetizing. The coup de grace came at the evening meal, where all in-house labor and that included us, were invited to share the master's table. Sounds good, but was it?

The family members and the farm manager and his family, would sit close to the head of the very large table that seated some thirty people. Frits and I, being the least significant of this enlarged family, sat at the very end. Food was served from the top down and although there always was time for second helpings close to the head of the table, by the time we were ready for some more, Mr. Bjornson would get up and declare the meal over and done with. Had it not been for our good relations with the kitchen staff, we would have starved as we did during the war years.

After two weeks of this we had enough, collected our wages — that were not bad — and moved to the big city of Copenhagen, ready to spend it all on good times and beer. We saw a lot of the Tivoli Beer Gardens, sleeping in parks and sometimes at the homes of people we met during our roaming through the city. After a couple of days of this, while our cash reserves dwindled at a rapid rate, Frits, being the more thoughtful of the two of us, suggested we move on to Sweden.

Sweden, just across The Sound, can be reached by ferry multiple times per day. At Helsingor, a little north of Copenhagen, the distance is less than ten miles. Following my six months stay in Denmark during 1946, I still had fairly decent command of the Danish language and as Norwegian is very close to Danish, we decided to go to Norway. We wanted to witness the midnight sun. As we had started our trip during July, about a month after the summer solstice, we had to go some 1000 miles north to see the sun at midnight. We did not quite make it but came close.

In Sweden, we found the going a little slower than we had been used to. The Swedes, not having suffered German occupation, were a little spoiled and not too keen on loading a couple of rather dirty louts with backpacks into their fancy little Volvos. In fact, some of the lifts we did get in Sweden were from foreigners. It took us a couple of days to cross Sweden into Norway. There we immediately felt at home again, but also in Norway the going was slow in the beginning. There was little traffic and once north of Oslo it almost came to a complete stop. To hitchhike you need many cars, as even under the best conditions few people will bother to stop and pick up two bums.

We had been stuck for most of the day without any luck when we saw two cars coming up the road at high speed. The first one was a small Mercedes and the second the latest sports model Volvo. The Mercedes flew past but the Volvo stopped. The guy behind the wheel shouted to get in quick as he was racing the Mercedes and didn't want to lose time. We piled in, I in the mini rear seat and Frits in the front. We were off in seconds, our driver explaining that he was racing the Mercedes for fun.

"I have a long way to go and a little racing will reduce the boredom and shorten the time. Where are you two going?"

I said, "We are on our way to Narvik to see the midnight sun. How far can you take us?'

Our driver then said, "You are in luck. I'm going almost all the way to a small town about one hundred miles south of Narvik."

To understand each other we had to shout as we were racing with a roaring engine and tires that complained loudly round every curve in the road. Since we were driving through a mountainous region, there were many bends. Bends of the hairpin and hair-raising kind. After about thirty minutes of this, we got the Mercedes in our sights again. Norman, our host and driver, assured us we would soon overtake him.

"Bah, the guy does not know how to drive in these mountains, but what else can you expect from a Swede?"

Sure enough, it wasn't long before we overtook him on a totally blind corner. Norman must have been clairvoyant and *saw* that nothing was coming from the other side. From there on the going was easy. Norman didn't really slow down much after winning his race, and as there was very little traffic in either direction we made good progress. He told us he was a dentist, lived in a small fishing village with a population of about 2000 and that he had been to Oslo to divorce his wife. According to him, he was *free at last* and had the full intention to enjoy his new status. While telling us this he occasionally took a swig from a flask he had stashed in the inside pocket of his jacket. He did offer us some as well and Frits, trying to be polite, took a careful sip that was followed by a coughing fit. This to the amusement of Norman, who reminded us that we were too young to drink. According to Frits the stuff tasted like gasoline.

I knew that in those days prohibition was the law in Norway. Alcoholic beverages were available in restaurants but one could not buy wines or liquor for consumption at home. Beer was available, but rationed. I asked Norman where and how he obtained his supplies. He explained that as a dentist he received a monthly allocation of pure alcohol for the cleaning of his instruments. Instruments could just as well be disinfected in an autoclave and he was therefore never short of a good drink. Good, being a relative concept. He did cut it down a little with beverages such as tea, coffee and fruit juice, his favorite being a fifty-fifty mix with tea. We were in very good hands.

After we had gone almost five hundred miles, Norman decided to call it quits for the day and pulled up in front of a little hotel. He booked himself a room and as we were short of cash, we made do with our sleeping bags under a nice tree on the lawn. The sun went under for only a couple of hours, but we slept like logs, nearly as well as the logs that were stacked up nearby to become next winter's firewood.

In the morning Norman invited us in and bought us a gigantic breakfast that was served with coffee. Coffee, doctored with some of his medical ethanol, a great way to start a day of driving on treacherous mountain roads. A couple of hours into the drive north, Norman told me he needed a break and could I take over. He, like the German General, did not ask to see a driver's license.

The rest of the way to Rosvik, his village, I drove with Frits in the passenger seat and Norman snoring loudly on the backseat. Rosvik, at that time a sleepy fishing village, lies about one hundred miles north of the Arctic Circle. On our arrival Norman asked us to stay the night at his home, a nice old wooden structure where he lived with his somewhat demented and alcoholic father.

Initially we had planned to travel all the way to Narvik, but as we had no money left, we asked Norman if he could help us find some work in Rosvik. He was a member of the city council and the next day we were put to work chopping up a very large pile of logs that had to be hand sawn into twenty-four inch sections and then chopped down to furnace sized fire-wood. Not with the help of a wood-splitter. It all had to be done by hand. We contracted to do the entire pile for, what seemed to us, a fabulous amount of money. The work was very hard and painful during the first few days but we completed the job in three weeks, developing some serious muscles in our arms and shoulders and hard calluses in our hands. We also made more money than either of us had ever had access to. We thought ourselves rich and had the best time of our lives.

Norman had invited us to stay at his house for the duration, and as he refused to take any money, we went grocery shopping and bought all the beer that household could consume. The old man took care of at least a dozen or so per day. Beer was rationed, but it was amply available on the black market.

Inhabitants of this arctic region with its long dark winters have a way of celebrating the long summer days and celebrate we did. Hardly a day went by without some party or festivity. In these parts and shortly after the war, foreigners were rare and as a result, we were treated with friendly curiosity and kindness. The girls went absolutely crazy over us. Green and inexperienced as we were, we were both subjected to some overdue sex education at the hands — and not only the hands — of a number of the local belles. I lost my virginity there, was practically raped, and although initially a little shocked, enjoyed it tremendously. Frits had a similar experience and told me he had been afraid she was going to bite it off.

Apart from being attacked one night by Norman's old man, who in a sort of delirium came at me during the early morning hours with a hand-ax, our three weeks in Rosvik passed peacefully. I escaped the assault by jumping naked from my bedroom window on the second floor. I remember clearly that Norman's girlfriend, who had woken up because of the racket the old man made, stood on the balcony of her room watching me with curiosity. By the time I got back into the house the old man had passed out on the living room floor. There was never a dull moment in Rosvik!

All good things must come to an end. It was time we started traveling back towards home. Unless we met another maniac like Norman it might be slow going. And it was— there was hardly any traffic and what was there was mostly local. Some of the rides we accepted were for a couple of miles only. We spent ten days to get to Oslo—rode in at least twenty different vehicles and walked many, many miles. As we had money in our pockets, we spent it freely. Why sleep outside if you can afford to stay in the local inn?

It took us another couple of weeks to traverse Sweden, Denmark and Germany. After a total of nearly ten weeks, we arrived back in Groningen, flat broke, hungry and in extreme need of a bath. A couple of days earlier, our parents, not having received a single sign of life from either of us during that entire time, had reported us missing. Interpol was looking all over Europe for two boys. Had they been looking for two young men, they might have found us. Boys we were no more.

Herman Thorbecke

Chapter 5

EMIGRATING TO AFRICA

We were married very young. I was eighteen and Fredy, nineteen, neither of us anywhere near grown up. We were children, but at least that decision we made together. When she became pregnant, my father who was an MD, offered to make arrangements for an abortion. We thought about it for some time and discussed it with my uncle, also an MD, who was to perform the procedure. The fact that abortions were still illegal at that time in the Netherlands did not affect our decision. We believed we loved each other, wanted to get married and have the child. And what a good thing that was. I cannot imagine my life without Bert, my first-born son.

At the time we were both still in college, I in my second year of a four year course that taught me the elements of the agricultural sciences, she in her final year in hotel management. I had been a rather mediocre student before, but in spite of continuing to enjoy my life as a student, I did develop some sense of responsibility. I studied hard and graduated magna cum laude and first in my class.

The second decision that we made jointly was to

33

emigrate, leave Holland with its wet and miserable climate. This country had only negative memories for us. For me, as I had grown up during German occupation and later, after the war, in the middle of economically depressed conditions. For Fredy, as she was almost a stranger in that country, having lived in Indonesia until she was thirteen years old. Not that her life there had been a picnic. She spent nearly four of those years in a Japanese concentration camp, separated from her family and coming close to dying of starvation.

We were therefore determined to go and live somewhere far away from that wet little country and our relatives, who kept treating us like the children we really were, always interfering with unwelcome, but mostly sensible suggestions. Like for instance—go back to school for postgraduate studies. No way was I going back to school, having to live more years on the minimal stipend that our parents allowed us. I was ready to go out into the world and take care of myself and my family. Keep in mind that in those days there were no fast-food restaurants where students could find work, flipping burgers. Neither were there any other part-time jobs other than seasonal work on farms. I had my share of those—digging up sugar beets and cleaning pigsties.

I started applying for overseas positions and was soon offered a job as an assistant plantation manager for a Dutch rubber company on the island of Sumatra, Indonesia. However, that never happened as the Indonesian Government, just having freed itself from Dutch colonialism, refused to give us visas. I believe they wanted the world to know: "No more Dutchmen running anything in our country!" That was a great disappointment for both of us, but particularly for Fredy, who had been looking forward to going back to that beautiful country of her origins.

The next best offer I received was from the South African Department of Agriculture in the animal husbandry division. A subject well outside the area of my agricultural training, but that did not matter to me. They offered us our ticket out of The Netherlands and into a tropical environment.

They paid a subsistence salary, but that did not bother us either as it was certainly going to be more than what was handed out to us by our parents. I also had to sign a three-year contract. For that, they would reimburse all travel expenses. No time was wasted. I was never a procrastinator and we agreed to sail from Rotterdam on a Union Castle Line ship, the Capetown Castle, during March of 1957.

No, we did not spend much time thinking about this move that would eventually mature us and play such a decisive role in molding us into adults. Both of us wanted to get away, and both of us had totally unrealistic expectations. I had just finished reading Hemingway's *The Green Hills of Africa*, a little book he wrote about his safaris and big game hunting trips in Kenya. I was ready for some of that. The possibility that my hunting experiences, if I may refer to them in those terms, might not be anywhere near as glamorous, never occurred to me.

As for Fredy's expectations, I can only guess and believe she was hoping to find a tropical heaven, similar to the one she grew up in, on the slopes of the Javanese mountains, where her dad had been the manager of a tea plantation.

Both families assembled at the docks in Rotterdam to wish us farewell and I suspect in the case of some individuals, good-riddance. I still have a little Kodak print, showing us, with my rather glum looking parents. The ones really smiling were Fredy, pregnant with our second child, and me. Smiling, because we were full of hope and did not know what we were in for. Poor little Bert was close to tears, as he realized he was going to be separated from his granddad, also named Bert, with whom he had developed a close relationship. If we had asked him at that time, "Bert, do you want to come with us to a far-away country, where we know no-one?" his answer would most certainly have been a resounding, "No, I want to stay here, where I know everyone!"

Departure from Rotterdam

But, of course, nobody asked little Bert and that is just as well. Were we to ask little children their opinion about the making of life-changing decisions, they would mostly prefer the status-quo, and no progress would ever be made. However, Bert thrived in South Africa. He loved the animals and the people, particularly the blacks. One of his first questions about his new environment there was, "Why are the black people so beautiful?"

Yes, my son and I had many things in common. In spite of the stringent apartheid laws, forbidding all social contact between whites and blacks, I did break those rules every opportunity I was given.

It took the Capetown Castle almost three weeks to sail to the city of its naming. We made three stops on the way. The first one was at Madeira, the romantic Portuguese island famous for its wine. We spent an entire day sightseeing, of which I remember preciously little—most likely due to sampling the local product more amply than I should have. Fredy told me later that the place was gorgeous. The next stop was St. Helena, where we also had a full day of sight-seeing. We visited Napoleon's famous home. I remember thinking that it was not really that bad a place for a quiet retirement, the way it was situated on top of a nice hill with a fabulous view. But then I suppose, if you are a Napoleon, you are never ready for a peaceful and isolated withdrawal from power, fame and glory.

After returning Fredy and Bert to our cabin on the Capetown Castle, there was plenty of time for another visit to the Island and one of its drab little bars. While drinking some of the local brews, I ended up having an argument and a fistfight with one of the locals, who had taken offence at my referring to him as one of the "natives." It was later explained to me that under British colonialism, natives were substandard people that could not trace their origins to the British Isles. A matter of linguistic misunderstanding on my part, for which I believe I should have been excused, considering my then very limited knowledge of the English language. When I tried to explain myself by pointing out that I thought of myself as a native of Holland, he was not having any of it and attempted to punch me. As he was more intoxicated than I was, he missed and I did not.

The local police were called and the outcome of that little excursion was my being escorted back to the ship in handcuffs, a disgraceful spectacle that my little family was fortunately spared from having to witness. I swear to you that this was the only time I was ever arrested. On St Helena of all places. I was a prisoner on St Helena. Me and Napoleon. However, when it came to visiting Ascension Island, our next and final stop on the way to our destination, I was prohibited from leaving the ship by the purser. On Bert's query why that was so, I explained that only British subjects were allowed to visit the island. He did not think that was fair and I fully agreed.

This little world of ours has many fabulous ports, but in my opinion few, if any, can match what is offered by a landfall in the shadow of the Table Mountain of Cape Town, the most southern city of the African continent. On our early morning approach to the port, dolphins, penguins, and seals accompanied us. Everything seemed so perfect and although the three of us were somewhat overwhelmed with the confusion of the debarkation and the reality of our arrival, we were happy and hopeful.

Our tourist days were supposed to be over. The

instructions were clear—we were to catch the evening train, leaving that same day for Bloemfontein in the Orange Free State. I disagreed and decided that we needed at least one day to recuperate from the arduous ocean voyage. After safe depositing our luggage at the train station, we wandered around the city for some time, admiring the sights and the people. People of many races and origins inhabit Cape Town. We found every possible shade of skin color represented there. From full-blooded, pitch-black African to blue-eyed, lily-white Irish and everything in between. Apart from the African and European features, we recognized Indian and Malay characteristics. The Dutch, during their days of colonizing the Cape, imported willing labor from the Dutch East Indies, now Indonesia. Then came the British and they brought the Indians. I believe there are more beautiful women in Cape Town than in any other city in the world. You do not have to take my word for it, but I did do some research.

Arrival with Table Mountain in background

We ended up at Seapoint on the waterfront and spent the night there at the Millroy Hotel. It was obvious that it had seen better days, but to us it was heaven and we enjoyed a memorable evening. For me the highlight of that evening occurred when I went down to the bar by myself for a quick nightcap. I got into a pleasant conversation with a young couple who told me a lot about my newly adopted country and made me feel good about myself and our resolve to come to this part of the world. Their stories really helped, and relieved me of some of my anxiety and uncertainty about our move to Africa.

It was the following morning that I realized they had also relieved me of my wallet, that had contained most of the money we had brought. Fortunately that was not very much, but more than we could afford to lose.

The train-ride to Bloemfontein, with many stops on the way, took some eighteen hours but was otherwise uneventful. I was not very happy and Fredy's repeated reproofs and blame for having lost most of our little capital totally screwed up my day. The really annoying part was that without any doubt, she was right.

All in all not a very promising beginning.

Chapter 6

STEAM TRAINS AND HYENAS

In spite of the rather inauspicious beginning, we quickly settled into our new environment. After a short stint in a boarding house, one of my new colleagues told me about a small house that was available on his farm some ten miles out of town, near a pretty river with beautiful trees and very low rent. The fact that it had no electricity was a bit of a problem, but we soon learned to make do with romantic oil lamps and a smelly kerosene stove.

Overall, the place after a thorough cleaning and some painting was quite comfortable. There were three bedrooms, an enormous kitchen and a nice screened porch. Martine, our daughter was born there and as soon as we moved in, the third bedroom was made ready for her arrival. Water came from a well with a windmill, refrigeration from an oil-fired contraption that at the best of times only managed to keep things lukewarm. Shortly after we arrived, a number of young local women came by to offer their services as house-maids. In those days people were willing to work for board and lodging plus a small wage. Fredy appointed Anna, a statuesque, slender Basutu with demure eyes and a shy smile. She told us that she had a husband who treated her badly — the reason she preferred not to go home on her off days. Bert soon learned to love Anna and I have to admit, so did I.

Our first home in South Africa

After a short training period in Bloemfontein, the capital of what was then called The Orange Free State and now simply the Free State, I learned about the details of my occupation for the next three-year contract. I was to travel around the state, making monthly visits to about twenty dairy farms, where I was to inspect the cattle, record milk production and herd development. I was also to carry out semen collection and distribution thereof for artificial insemination. Distribution is easy; collection from prime bulls, weighing around 2000 pounds, is a whole other story. . .

Although I am sure you would like to hear more about that subject and wonder, as I still do, how I managed and survived those encounters, it will have to be the theme of another tale. Let me just say that had it not been for quick reflexes and much good fortune, I would not have been here to tell about it in my current, unmarred physical condition.

As the South African Government was either not very affluent or generous or most likely both, I was not allowed a car for my travels. The monthly trip to these farmers I was to make by train. At the beginning of each month, I mailed every one of them a notification that I would be arriving at the nearest railway station on a certain day and time. They were then responsible for picking me up, housing me for the night and dropping me off at the same station the next day. By visiting one farmer per day, I completed my rounds in a matter of three weeks or less and had at least one week off each month. That is if everything went according to plan. Unfortunately, that was not always the case.

During the time this event unfolded — it was 1959, I believe — most of the trains in South Africa were using steam as the only form of propulsion. Good old steam trains that choo-chooed along on narrow railways at top speeds of some sixty miles per hour with numerous stops on the way. Let me assure you that these provincial trains were nothing like the famous and luxurious Blue Train that traveled, practically non-stop, from Cape Town to Johannesburg. No, these local trains were relics dating back to the beginning of the twentieth century. They were mainly for the transportation of freight with one or two passenger cars for whites and a couple of cars for Africans. Apartheid was very much the rule of the land.

The dairy farms that I was to visit monthly were located in the southeastern part of the Orange Free State around the towns of Jagersfontein, Koffiefontein and Phillippolis. The latter city during the eighteen-forties was the

43

scene of an historic fight between the Boers and Griquas. This tribe of Africans was disputing the Boer settlements on their lands and they had the support of the British, who were masters at the art of "divide and rule."

That part of the country consists of a highland plateau at an elevation of some 5000 to 6000 feet above sea level. The winters are dry and cold with night temperatures regularly below freezing and this being the Southern Hemisphere, the coldest months are July and August. Most people that have not visited those parts do not associate Africa with freezing weather, but be not mistaken—it can get very cold in the highlands.

Pickaninnies "dressed" for the cold

It was during July that I had an unnerving encounter with a pack of brown hyenas. Until that day, my current trip around the farms had gone off without a hitch. Some of my traveling had been done at night and during the bitterly cold nights the train compartments were barely heated and most uncomfortable. To bring some relief the train conductor provided passengers with large hot water bottles to warm their feet.

These local trains stopped at all little stations and some of the halts were nothing other than a crossroad with a water tank for replenishing the water needed by the steam engines. It was at one of these stops in the middle of nowhere that my next farmer client, Jaap Viljoen, was supposed to pick me up. When I got off the train with all my equipment, Mr. Viljoen had not yet arrived but as he had on previous visits always shown up sooner or later I was not concerned. It was a relatively mild and sunny late afternoon. I had something to read and sat on my cases patiently awaiting his arrival.

South African Railways in action

Now, as I mentioned earlier, this was truly the middle

45

of nowhere. The road that intersected the railway at this point was nothing more than a narrow dirt road, and the Viljoen farm was some ten miles away with no other homesteads within miles. After I had waited about an hour and no one had shown up or passed by since my arrival, I started to get concerned. I knew with certainty that he had been notified, first by mail and as that was not always reliable, also by phone. I myself had called him two days earlier to remind him.

The sun was rapidly on its way down and so was the temperature, which could be expected to drop well below freezing that night. I was also getting hungry and after gobbling down a sandwich that had been left over from lunch, I started out to collect combustible materials for a fire. That was easier said than done, as the veldt in those parts is practically bare of vegetation other than grass and some low shrubs. Searching around the railway water tank, I was fortunate to come across a pile of discarded lumber, apparently left behind after the tank and its support had been constructed. There were also some pieces of coal scattered along the track. I collected what I could and piled it close to a copse of shrubs that offered some protection against a cold breeze that had started to blow from the south.

In the meantime, the sun had gone down. At those latitudes, the sun does not linger. It sets and in a matter of twenty minutes, it's night. The only illumination would come from the stars that soon started to appear in all their glory and in numbers that one can only observe at such altitudes and away from the contamination of city lights. It was getting cold and after starting a fire, I put on a second layer of clothing. My sleeping bag that I carried, to keep warm on overnight trips on the cold trains, would also come in very handy.

By now I was resigned to spending the night out in the open. I was hungry but not thirsty as a couple thousand gallons of water were at my disposal in the tank. In spite of everything, I was actually starting to enjoy my little camping adventure. If only I had had some steaks to cook over my campfire. Instead, I smoked some Lucky Strikes and was confident that the fire's glow would serve to keep me warm and safe from attack by the local wildlife.

There was some reason for concern, as I knew the region to be the habitat of some survivors of what used to be a thriving lion population. And, there were of course all sorts of different antelope, wild dogs and hyenas. I was not too worried. I had my fire, a revolver that I always carried on these trips and an abundance of confidence that soon proved to be mostly unwarranted.

I must have dozed off shortly after I had built up the fire with plenty of wood and some coal. It seemed I had only been asleep for minutes, when I awoke from a dream about some girls laughing at me. They were laughing loudly because I was naked and shivering from the cold. I was up and on my feet in a hurry, realized I wasn't naked but chilled to the bone and immediately piled some more wood on the fire that had almost expired. As I was occupied with this, the laughing voices still echoed in my head. Very disturbing for a young man who had always thought of himself as a ladies' man—this feeling of being open for ridicule and actually being laughed at by...

Exactly who or what was laughing at me? Now,

suddenly wide awake, I recognized the quarreling, whining and yapping for what it was and knew I was being "laughed" at by a pack of hyenas. Locals later told me that the brown hyenas, which occur in those parts, don't "laugh" like the spotted hyenas one finds further north. Well, let me assure you that in my dream it sure sounded like laughter — loud and scornful.

Just recently, I had been reading a description of the hyena's lifestyle and habits. Immediately it came to mind (that troublesome mind) that they really are not the cowardly scavengers they are often purported to be. They have been known to actually attack and chase lions away from their kill. If that were so — and I did have my doubts, as I had found that report in the Readers Digest — I might be in trouble.

First things first. I unpacked my revolver and fired a couple of shots in the general direction (all around me) from which the "laughter" had come. After a couple of minutes of total silence, I was rewarded with more noise from the gallery, which I interpreted as, "You must be kidding. We are going to have you for dinner, as soon as we have built up our resolve and appetite."

It was just after midnight now and I realized I was not going to get much sleep until they would vanish at daybreak. Hyenas are a nocturnal species that are rarely seen in action during daytime. I piled more wood on the fire and every time they seemed to come nearer, I got up waving a firebrand. That was effective in driving them back temporarily, but as time went by and I grew more tired, they appeared to come closer and closer. As the moon had come up, I could clearly see them slinking around, continuously yapping and snarling at each other. In a way, that was reassuring as now I could keep my eye on them. They kept circling in a pack, more or less staying together and that too was helpful, as I had no eyes in the back of my head. All the same, I kept hearing and imagining them getting at me from all directions.

After what seemed longer than my entire life, the stars were starting to fade and soon the lovely sun, that reassuringly warm and friendly sun illuminated the horizon. In no time at all the hyenas vanished and soon I started to feel the warmth of the sunrays caressing my chilled bones. I had made it and I was deadly tired and soon fell asleep in the glow of the early morning. And again I had a dream. This time the telephone was ringing and I was frantically groping around, trying to pick it up. Before I did find the phone, I heard the person on the other end shouting, "Hello Baas, can I help you?"

"Yes, you can. I am so glad to hear your voice!"

This I said as I was waking up, seeing one of the kindliest faces I have ever encountered in my entire life. It belonged to a graying African, who was standing some paces away, looking very unsure of himself and ready to take off at the slightest provocation. Who knows what this crazy white man would be capable of? He was holding a bicycle with a gleaming bell on the handlebars, a bell he must have been ringing to call me on my dream phone.

I got up while he cautiously retreated several feet and I explained my predicament. I told him that I needed to get to the Viljoen farm. On hearing this he exclaimed, "I work for Baas Jaap and you are the Baas who comes to catch the bull piss. I will hurry to tell Baas Jaap that you have arrived. He

49

will come to get you with his motorcar."

So ended my little camping trip in the middle of Africa. Jaap Viljoen showed up in a matter of a few short hours, highly apologetic, assuring me that his wife was preparing a fabulous breakfast of lamb chops, eggs, mieliepap and peach jam. I just asked him to hurry, as I was very hungry.

Chapter 7

CHIEF MAKALO

While drinking a cup of Rooibos Tea, the other day, I was reminded of a short vacation we took during the winter of 1960. We spent a week in the beautiful city of Durban on the coast of Natal, a little paradise for people of all ages that love warm weather, the tropical beaches of the Indian Ocean and some of the best Indian food in the world.

It was on our drive back to Bloemfontein that I was first served a cup of Kalahari Rooibos Tee—Redbush Tea. It is an herbal tea extracted from the leaf tips of Aspalathus linearus, and is known in Afrikaans as Rooibos. It's delicious, with a sweet and penetrating aroma that is reminiscent of wild berries with a hint of Shiraz.

It was on this road trip home with my young wife, five-year old son, Bert and two-year old daughter, Martine that we had a memorable encounter. It was an early midwinter morning during August with temperatures close to freezing. The countryside looked barren and bleak, the overall color, a rusty brown as a result of the soil's high iron content. We had just left a little motel in Bethlehem, traveling south along an almost deserted road through the Orange Free State, which lies mostly at an elevation of some 5000 feet. It is a flat plateau, with here and there a small, table-topped hill, which the locals refer to as Koppies and that resemble the famous Table Mountain of the Cape of Good Hope. Just a lot smaller.

As we were coming around one of these hills, we saw a tall Basutu wearing the traditional colorful blanket draped around his shoulders and on his head, the distinctive, conical straw hat the area is known for. He carried a small bundle and walked along the side of the road. As we overtook him, he waved at us with his beautiful hat.

We had plenty of opportunity to observe him as the old 1950 model Vauxhall, the first car I had ever owned, was only capable of topping fifty miles per hour when going downhill. Since we were going uphill, we were chugging along at a lot less than that. As we passed him, my son, who was sitting up front with me, remarked, "Daddy, that poor man must be very cold. Can we take him with?"

Bert on the old Vauxhall, ready to go for a ride

Although, we had been in South Africa for only a couple of years, we had already absorbed enough of the "white-man-in-Africa" attitudes to make us think twice about picking up a black man in the middle of nowhere. I had slowed down a little and now my wife, who was relaxing on the back seat with little Martine, agreed with our son and said, "Yes, why not, let's take him with, he's probably on his way to Basutu Land and that is quite a long way to walk."

I must admit I still had some reservations, but decided to at least stop and speak to him. If he did not seem friendly, we could always just let him continue on foot. As we had come to a stop several hundred feet past him, I put the old Vauxie in its whining reverse gear and made my way back to where he had stopped in the road. He was in his late twenties and at least six feet tall, which is unusual for the natives of that region. He smiled openly, showing a perfect set of very white teeth and while holding his hat against his chest, greeted us joyfully.

"Good morning, Baas, good morning, Madam. It is very cold today. Is the Baas going far?"

"We are on our way to Maseru and then to Bloemfontein. What is your name and where are you going?"

"My name is Makalo. Makalo Moeketsi. I am son of Chief Moeketsi and am the Induna in the gold mines. I am going home to my family in Leribe."

He spoke with clear diction and with apparent pride about his name, which meant nothing to us at the time. We later learned that his father became the Minister of Agriculture of Basutu Land a number of years later. Leribe,

53

now known as Hlotse, was a small settlement and mission school in the northern part of his country, just a few miles from the border with South Africa. A couple of French missionaries started it during the nineteenth century.

"Well, Makalo, would you like to come with us to Leribe?" I asked him.

"Yes, Baas. Thank you, Baas."

I got out of the car, helped him tie his bundle to the roof-carrier, and then told him to get into the front seat with my son, who refused to sit in the back with his mom and sister. Once settled in the front with Bert on his knee he now asked my son, "And what is your name, young Basie?"

"My name is Bert and my daddy's name is Herman and he is also a chief."

I have no clue how he came up with that, but Makalo found it very amusing and gave forth a truly heart-warming basso laugh. He then told us that he had gone to the mission school in Leribe, had been working for the gold mines for several years, and had just been promoted to the position of Induna, in charge of a group of fifty workers. On my question why he worked so far from home, he explained that there was no work in his country that paid decent wages and that the family farm was well taken care of by the women, while most of the men worked in the mines.

photo by Joseph Gill www.worldglobetrotters.com

Firewood transport in Lesotho

We had at least another fifty miles to go and during the following hour had plenty of time to talk. And talk he did, telling us that he had been married for five years and had a son of Bert's age, that he came home once per year for a month and that tomorrow his brother was getting married. All the while he had my son on his knee, occasionally addressing himself to Bert with questions about the games he liked to play. Calling him Bertie, he asked my son if he knew how to ride a pony.

"Yes, I know how to ride a pony, you just sit on top and hold on to his mane," was Bert's reply.

In fact, during our vacation in Durban, he had for the first time in his life sat on a pony. Makalo laughed loudly and then told him that there was more to riding a pony and invited Bert to come and visit him on his farm, where he would teach him how to ride. I do not remember the exact moment, but I think it was at that stage of the conversation that he saved my son's life.

The Vauxhall, like most cars of that era, had front doors that opened forward. Suicide doors, we used to call them. Bert had been told never to touch the door handles, but in his excitement about the prospect of riding ponies on Makalo's farm, he must have held on to the handle and unlatched the door. As soon as the wind grabbed the opening door, it swung outwards violently and had it not been for Makalo's lightning reaction, snatching him by the back of his shirt, my son would have flown out with the door and landed on the pavement. Even at only forty-five miles per hour, it would have most likely killed or seriously maimed him.

We came to a stop and all I could do to vent my fear and shock was to shout and get angry with little Bert, who promptly burst into tears. This is where this black man showed his breeding and in my eyes became Chief Makalo.

"Baas, please not to be angry with Bertie, it was my fault. I should have prevented it. He was sitting with me and I should have stopped him touching the door. It is my responsibility only."

I then told him, "Makalo you are not at fault. You just saved the life of my son and I am deeply grateful. Please never say it was your fault. It is because of you that he is unharmed and alive. Thank you, Chief Makalo."

At this Makalo was all smiles again and assured me that he was not a chief. His father was the chief and I should please not call him so, as it was not proper. I would have hugged the man, but in those days, you did not hug black men. In fact, as this was very much an Anglo environment, you did not hug any men. South Africans gave firm handshakes and saluted each other. I tend to believe that things have changed since Mandela put his stamp on the country. In fact I have seen him do hugs. What a man this Mandela! At any rate, I shook Makalo's hand. I shook it very firmly.

There is not much else to report. We dropped him off at his Kraal, just outside Leribe. He introduced us, with great formality, to his wife, who was quite beautiful and dressed in the traditional manner with a colorful headscarf and a fine, Merino wool blanked with a pattern of corn ears, draped around her shoulders. She served us tea, "Rooibos tee" she called it, and told us it was very healthy. We also got to know his son, who was about Bert's age. Makalo then called someone to bring a pony and asked for our permission to give Bert his first riding lesson. He put both boys on the pony together and trotted them around for twenty minutes.

The little detour into Lesotho became the highlight of our vacation. I remember this black man very well and to me he always was and will be Chief Makalo!

Herman Thorbecke

Traditional blankets are part of the national dress.

Chapter 8

A BULL TERRIER NAMED JOCK

My son Bert was seven years old when he asked me to get him a dog. A dog just like Jock of the book we had read together.

You may not be familiar with Percy Fitzpatrick's famous South African classic, *Jock of the Bushveld,* about the bull terrier that shared his master's life in South Africa. This book is a little jewel that remains as fresh and exciting as the day it was written, its writer personally inspired by his friend, Rudyard Kipling.

I read parts of the book to Bert and must admit that I was just as smitten with the idea of getting a bull terrier puppy as he was. It wasn't long before my travels among the local farmers brought me to one that had a fabulous litter of these rather rambunctious dogs. Both parents were purebred, brindled bull terriers of well over sixty pounds each. Baas, the male had been a show dog and apart from being a very effective watchdog, was fully trained as a hunting companion.

The farmer told me, "I have always kept a couple of these terriers on the farm. They are great for keeping vermin and other nuisance animals such as hyenas and stray dogs at bay. They are totally fearless—fearless to the extent that one sometimes wonders how smart they really are. I mean, what sensible dog would attack a pack of hyenas? Well, Baas will and has and the amazing part is that he always manages to run them off."

I said, "That sounds very much like that brave bull terrier from the famous book *Jock of the Bushveld* written by Fitzpatrick." He then told me in Afrikaans and a rather gruff tone, "Ek lees geen Engelse boeke nie." (I don't read English books).

I now pointed out, "But I'm sure it must have been translated into Afrikaans."

"Maar dit is nog steeds 'n Engelse boek." (But it still is an English book).

This served as a clear warning that it was time to change the subject. After the Boer War (1899 to 1902), during which the British invented concentration camps, many Afrikaans people, understandably, still wanted nothing to do with them.

At the time of my visit, Baas's pups were only six weeks old, but already showed some rather ferocious behavior. As they continuously squabbled and fought among themselves, one wondered where the line between playing and fratricide was drawn. They went for the throat with their needle-sharp puppy teeth and one would not dare put his hand in there to separate them.

On coming home, I reported to Bert and his mother about my find and expressed my doubt about the suitability of these terriers as family pets. The more I told Bert about them, the more he liked the idea of getting one.

"Dad, that's just like Jock in the book we read. I don't want some sweet little lap-dog. Please, Daddy. Please!"

Thinking that making their acquaintance would temper his enthusiasm, particularly if he were to get an intro to the sharp teeth of these "lovely" puppies, I told Bert, "Well all right, we will go together to look at them, but remember they are very aggressive and you need to be careful not to get bitten."

"Don't worry Dad. I'm sure they won't bite me."

Initially, there had been a total of seven pups, four dogs and three bitches. At the time of our joint visit to the farm, there were only three left, two females and a little male that had been the runt of the litter. On our arrival, the little guy ran straight for Bert, climbing all over him, licking his face and generally letting the world know that he had found his *master*. There was no doubt in my mind that this would be our dog. Neither was there any doubt in Bert's, who announced, "We'll call him Jock, just like Jock of the Bushveld."

That same day Jock came home with us and soon he and Bert were inseparable. Jock adjusted well and other than chewing up every shoe that he managed to get hold of, he did not do too much damage. He was a cute little dog, brindled gray-brown, with one ear erect, while the other flopped over his left eye. He did not stay little for long though. Jock grew like cabbage. When we brought him home he did not put more than five pounds on the scale, but boy did that dog have an appetite. He ate like a wolf and it was not long until he weighed a solid sixty pounds. The little runt had become a big, hefty bull terrier, solid muscle and bone, strong as an ox and beginning to show signs of his real character and disposition. Early on, it became very obvious that he did not like other dogs. Bitches he would tolerate, particularly if in heat. Males he invariably attacked and chased off the property.

Jock, ready for action

We lived on a small farm some ten miles from Bloemfontein. Bert went to school in town and as there were other kids nearby that went to the same school, parents clubbed together and shared the driving. We (that is my wife, as I was away a lot) did the driving in an old Chevy pick-up truck that had room in the front for her, Bert and three of his school mates, if they squeezed closely together.

Our day of the week for doing the driving was Wednesday and it soon became a habit for Jock to hop in the back of the pick-up for the ride to school, where he would say his goodbyes with an effusion of hugs and kisses, of which the other children also received a fair share. Jock just loved people and children in particular.

He would reluctantly get back on the truck for the ride home, where for the remainder of the day, like on all other school days, he would sulk and bide his time until it was the moment for Bert to come home again. This routine was broken when my wife noticed one Wednesday that Jock, who invariably would ride on the truck to pick up the kids after school, was nowhere to be found. This was unusual and worrisome, but my wife had no other choice than to leave him behind, all the while wondering where he could be and how Bert would take his sudden disappearance.

Well, she could have saved herself that apprehension, as on driving up to the entrance of the school who did she see waiting patiently at the door? Jock, of course. Apparently, he could not stand to wait the entire day and as he knew the way, he had decided to jog to school to visit Bert. A couple of minutes later school was out and Bert then told his mom that Jock had arrived just in time for the afternoon recess. All the kids had had a fantastic time playing with him. The good-natured principal told my wife that Jock had behaved in an exemplary manner, but all the same impressed on Bert and his mom that these visits should not become a habit, please.

From that day on, Jock had to be restrained on Wednesdays, as we assumed that the principal's admonitions had not been heard by Jock. The very next Wednesday he was locked in the screened veranda. On returning from delivering the children to school, my wife found an empty veranda with a large hole in the screen. Jock had simply jumped straight through. She immediately got back in the truck to return to school. A few miles down the deserted dirt road she saw him happily trotting along, tail up and waving in glad anticipation of his reunion with Bert at school.

Jock was elated to see her, thinking he was going to get a ride to school and without any reservations cooperated by jumping into the back of the old Chevy. Once in the back, my wife gave him a severe talking-to and tied him to his chain leash, as he would no doubt have escaped the moment he realized she was returning home.

The following Wednesday Jock was chained to a running cable that gave him ample opportunity to move along a stretch of the lawn. I happened to have that day off and after seeing him variously sulk and loudly complain about his confinement, I decided to experiment by letting him off his leash. He immediately made a move towards the gate and the road to town, continuously looking back at me and barking invitingly to please follow him.

I did, and on catching up, gave him a good shaking and told him in no uncertain terms that he was not allowed to leave the grounds. I then reinforced this further by repeatedly walking him to the gate and from there, sending him back to the house. Jock was a smart dog and took the lesson well. He had come of age and from that day on never left the yard unaccompanied, not even on Wednesdays. That day we celebrated by playing his favorite game—tug-of-war—during which he nearly pulled me off my feet. As an excuse, I offer that at that time of my life I only weighed 180 pounds.

Jock learned many things quickly, except that he needed to be more peaceful in his attitude towards other male dogs. It took us many months of interactive sessions with other dogs of many breeds and all sizes to get him to understand that they did not walk this earth to serve him as sparring partners and/or lunch. Eventually we managed to get him to desist from unprovoked attacks. There were however many ways Jock could be provoked and one of them was for dogs to shoulder him aside. You may have observed how dominant dogs have a way of approaching other dogs from the side and sort of pushing them out of the way. Any dog attempting to do this to Jock learned to regret it instantly. He would whirl around, grab them somewhere on the neck or throat, and not let go before having done serious harm.

This was a problem and it remained a problem throughout his life. As he got a little older he would mellow generally, but never would he allow another dog to lord it over him without expressing his clear displeasure — displeasure that often ended in the other animal needing some intensive medical attention, or worse.

It was about six months after the school episode that we moved to the big city of Johannesburg, where we lived in a nice house in a nice neighborhood, where most of our nice neighbors also had dogs, nice dogs. Nice, overfed Boxers and nice nervous Dobermans and let's not forget the Rhodesian Ridgebacks that in some ways could match Jock's abilities as real bush dogs. Why am I so dismissive of other breeds of dogs? Well, partly from chauvinism, and rightly or not, I was and now still am convinced that there is no breed of dogs better adapted to the African bush than is the bull terrier. Unlike most other dogs, they are not bred for good looks, but for endurance, persistence, courage and plain chutzpah — cheek combined with smarts.

You can well imagine the trouble we ran into after

65

moving into our new home in Joh-burg. I don't know how many dogs he scrapped with and how many vet bills I paid in the couple of years that we lived in that city. All of us, and that included the entire neighborhood, were therefore very relieved when I accepted an offer for a new position in the Northern Transvaal, far away from the big city, in the small town of Tzaneen.

And a small town it was in those days. It had one hotel, one doctor, one elementary school, but even that was too big for us and we decided to live a couple of miles out of town and were lucky to find a marvelous old home of some historic significance. It had been the home of Dr Siegfried Annecke, a biologist well known for his research on malaria during the pioneer days of the Letsitele Valley and the Tzaneen area.

The Annecke House, as it was known locally, sat in the middle of an estate of several acres of neglected but still beautiful gardens with enormous mango and avocado trees, as well as numerous orange, fig and passion fruit trees. And there were papayas and bananas galore. We had very little need to buy fruit. In fact, I don't think we ever did during the four years we lived there.

The house was several hundred yards from the road and on all sides surrounded by bush and more bush with its dense mopani shrubs, interspersed with wild fig trees, various acacia species and a number of others, the names of which now escape me. During the entire time I lived there and roamed the area, I never quite figured where the borders of the Annecke Estate were. In short, it was the perfect home for us, our three children and Jock.

Jock loved them and they loved Jock

Apart from Bert, there were his sister Martine, three years his junior and Rudy, our youngest son. They all loved that place with its many diversions and opportunities for play. Other than acres of space and the mystery of the African bush with its wildlife large and small — we even had a couple of giraffes visiting our lawn once — there was a concrete water reservoir. Its water was pumped up from the depths by an old-fashioned windmill that, after I replaced some failing parts, worked like a charm and kept our "swimming pool" filled with fresh, cool water, year-round. As the water was used to irrigate the garden, the pool was continuously replenished and never needed chemicals. Because of the absence of chlorine and such, we did have to share it with some other creatures like frogs, lizards and an occasional fruit rat that fell out of the giant mango tree that shaded our pool. Come to think of it, the rats seemed to frequent the pool more so during the really hot season. Perhaps they are more like us than we like to think, and enjoy having a nice cool swim now-and-then.

Jock decidedly did not like swimming. He would get into the river to retrieve, but never just for fun. He was the only one in the family that did not frequent the pool on a regular basis. The single time I did see him go in there voluntarily was while in pursuit of an invading and totally harmless little dog who attempted to escape Jock's aggressive attentions by jumping into the water. After a moment's hesitation, Jock followed him in and drowned the poor little pooch, as he had seen crocodiles do to their prey. Fortunately, the children were not around to witness that horrifying episode.

No, our dog was not a *gentledog* like the poodles that now enrich my life. Jock was from the bad side of town. Crude, sometimes outside nasty and not always honest, but true to his friends and family. One was glad to have Jock around during a scrape when things got hairy. And they did on a couple of occasions.

I told you before about Jock's prowess at the game of tug-of-war. Give him the end of a rope to pull and he would treat it as his worst enemy, never letting go and continuously shaking and jerking it, as though he were trying to break its spine. He practiced this "gift" by grabbing hold of the knot at the end of a rope that I had rigged from a large tree for the kids to swing on. Once he got hold of the rope, he would not let go whatever you did or however hard you swung him. His jaws would lock onto that knot as if it was the throat of some imagined enemy. Only total exhaustion would make him let go, but that might be after a long while. If my memory serves me right, his record stood at thirty minutes.

This ferocious ability and determination, coupled to his courage and love for his family, drove Jock to do life-saving things—first for his master Bert and later for me.

One of the world's most venomous snakes is the black mamba, the only black part of which is inside its mouth. The color of the skin is a silvery gray or even greenish. The slightest bite or even a scratch caused by this snake can be deadly. The effects set in very quickly and unless, the anti-serum is administered within a very short period, the victim's fate is sealed. Jock had on numerous occasions demonstrated his ability to deal with snakes expeditiously. He made no distinction between harmless and dangerous species. If confronted with one that did not slither away, as snakes usually will, he would deal with them promptly.

When Bert was eleven he and a friend, accompanied by Jock, had ventured a little further than usual into the bush in pursuit of a baby baboon that had strayed away from the pack. On crossing a small creek, they surprised and then were confronted by a large snake, some eight feet long. Mambas, like most snakes, will get out of the way unless cornered, but this one stood his ground and made a move towards them. It was then that Jock took over. He crouched down in his characteristic attack mode and quietly circled the snake, continuously changing direction, compelling the snake to follow his movements. Mambas are among the fastest snakes known and this one attempted to strike at Jock several times, missing him by inches, each time to be faced by Jock from a different angle. He finally lunged at the snake after its strike had failed for the final time and nabbed him just behind the head. Jock then gave this mamba the treatment he had practiced so many times with our rope swing.

The boys had retreated to a safe distance during the fight but Bert knew that even a dead Mamba's fangs, if touched, may cause serious problems. He ran forward as soon as the fight was over and restrained Jock from further tussling with the dead snake. He then suspended it over a stick and carried it home as a trophy. Our gardener, Phinias, was a good hand at skinning and he mounted it on a nice mahogany board.

Jock, with his intrepid and courageous action probably saved Bert and/or his friend from being attacked and poisoned by this most venomous of African snakes. From that day Jock could do no wrong in our household and as a result we may have spoiled him a little. To his further credit, he never did allow himself to soften up and become a fat, lazy good-for-nothing-sleep-on-the-porch type of dog. He kept practicing and working out on the swing, did his laps around the yard, chased vermin and uninvited visitors. I should have followed his lead and would now be in much better shape, perhaps.

It is a good thing that he did not succumb to our well-intended, but sorely misguided attempts at making his life that of the proverbial lap-dog, as was demonstrated when I joined a hunting party about a year later.

I was never particularly keen on this *sport*, but on occasion was invited to join hunting parties on some of the very large cattle farms in that part of the country. If I did accept these invitations, it was not with the idea of shooting animals, but more for the opportunity to walk and experience the bushveld close-up and at its best. Estates of thousands of acres and even 30,000 acres were not uncommon. Most of them were located in the more arid regions and often very near to some of the large game reservations one can find in the Northern Transvaal. As a result of that proximity these cattle farms were often plagued by an excess of game and in some instances by lions, leopards and hyenas—very unwelcome guests on a cattle farm. The Van Meters, whose farm bordered on the famous Kruger Park, had more than their fair share of these invaders.

Jock usually accompanied me into the bushveld. He was now a fully mature, six-year-old and had over the years picked up the etiquette of a joint hike in the bush. Joint, as there were more than just the two of us in the party. Besides people there were other dogs—dogs that were trained and experienced pointers and retrievers. Rule #1 of the etiquette required each dog to ignore the other dogs and to mind his own business, that is, his master. Rule #2 was to never advance ahead of the leader unless so instructed. As you may well understand, Jock had not totally become proficient at rule #1, but was making great strides of improvement. Even if he fully knew how to obey rule #2, he was a firm believer in the idea that rules are there to be broken.

Apart from the Van Meters, father and his three mature sons, there was one neighboring farmer, six native trackers and some four or five other dogs. The object of the exercise was to track down and shoot a stray lion that had repeatedly attacked and killed cattle on their farms. After driving out to the area where the culprit had last been seen, we prepared our gear and guns and were assigned a tracker each. We were then told to walk in an easterly direction towards the river, which formed the border between the farmlands and the nature reserve. We were to maintain a distance from each other of about a hundred yards. In the dense mopani bush, it would be difficult to keep track but if we lost touch with each other, we were under no circumstance to call out, as that would warn and chase our prey off.

As I was the least experienced of the hunters — the weakest link one might say — the Van Meters assigned me the most experienced tracker, Joseph, who understanding that I was not a real hunter wanted to know, "Can the Baas shoot?"

My assurance that I was an expert marksman did not seem to convince him, as he then said wishfully, "Perhaps we will not find the Simba."

I had read that one of the typical marks a lion might leave in the dry sandy soils is a semi-circular swept patch, made by the lion's tail as it lies and contemplates its next move. While we were walking through the bush, I kept a keen eye out for that particular "spoor" and sure enough, after only ten minutes on our bush-walk, I spied exactly that type of clue to the presence of the lion. Excitedly I drew the attention of the tracker to my discovery. Joseph, supposedly the expert and walking just ahead of me had totally overlooked this critical evidence. Yes, I know! I was still young, arrogant and a little stupid.

"Joseph," I said, while pointing out the incriminating evidence, "What sort of tracker are you, if you don't even recognize this very obvious spoor of the lion?"

After looking me up and down and lifting his eyes to

the heavens, as if he were saying a silent prayer, he said, "Hauk Baas, please let me do the tracking. She is not a lion's tail that did that, but this tired grass moving in the wind." While saying this he pointed to some tall reeds of grass, the heads of which leaned over and brushed the sand, indeed, as if it were a little tired.

I instantly recognized my mistake and suddenly realizing that I was totally out of my depth, asked Joseph if he could shoot and if so, would he like to hold the gun?

"Baas, what are you saying? You know I am not allowed to hold a gun. If the other Basies see me with a gun they will shoot *me* instead of the simba."

Photo by Joseph Gill www.worldglobetrotters.com

No need to shoot this "Lover Boy"

It was just at that moment that Jock changed his free and easy gait to his characteristic crouching stance, showing us that he had detected game in the vicinity. Joseph and I both noticed and we immediately stopped dead in our tracks while I motioned to Jock to stay behind. His ears were flat on his head and his tail in line with his spine while he made nervous little steps, restraining himself from rushing forward. We then moved ahead cautiously, wondering what was hiding in that dense bush just in front of us. Probably just an impala or some other small game?

Joseph, who had been leading, now let me go ahead and with good reason, as just as I noticed his reluctance to move forward, I heard, before I saw, a tawny shape bounce towards us from the bush some two-hundred feet ahead of us. I raised the gun, aimed, shot and missed. To my credit, I must mention that I did have the presence of mind to fire again. This time I must have grazed him, as it slowed him down, but only for a very short blink in time. The span between that moment and my freezing on the spot and Joseph's—smart fellow—run for the nearest tree, was infinitely short. It was just enough for Jock to realize that now was the right instant to disregard rule #2. He rushed ahead and challenged the yellow monster, easily six times his size and weight, armed with formidable teeth and claws. Simba hesitated briefly, only seventy-five feet from where I stood, frozen in time, but just long enough for Michael Van Meter, who had strayed closer to us in his search for the lion. Experienced hunter that he was, he took a quick bead and shot this old lion dead.

Michael fired his deadly round just a split second too late to save Jock's life. A violent swipe of the old warrior's left paw connected with Jock and broke his neck. It happened so quickly that I like to believe that Bert's faithful bull terrier never knew what hit him. Perhaps I am wrong and Jock was fully aware of what he was doing, but willingly gave his life. He lost his and I believe that he instinctively saved mine. According to Michael and Joseph, he sure as hell did. Had the lion not slowed down a little when Jock confronted him, Michael might not have had the opportunity to dispatch him in time — in time to prevent him from tearing me apart.

Bert was inconsolable but took pride from the fact that his Jock had been that brave. He observed, "You know, Dad, Jock had the heart of a lion."

We buried Jock with full bush honors on the Annecke Estate under a black slab of river rock. His epitaph: Here rests Jock, lion-hearted, always true to his master, but always his own Dog!

Herman Thorbecke

Chapter 9

A LOVE-CHILD IS CONCEIVED

One of the jobs I managed to secure, in my search for ever greener pastures, was as a technical representative with a company with the name Kynoch, a fertilizer manufacturer and subsidiary of African Explosives and Chemical Industries.

Explosives, in a country that virtually depended on gold and diamond mining, formed an essential element of industrial production. Nitrates are the corner stones of both explosives and fertilizers, hence the creation of Kynoch— initially, as a manufacturer of ammonium nitrate and other nitrogenous fertilizers, and later as a full-scale producer of both fertilizers and pesticides. As one of their technical reps, I was to go out among the farmers and act as a knowledgeable expert on the subject of crop nutrition and pest control. It was my job to represent the company's policy and recommend the products we sold.

I stuck to that line of work for the remainder of my years in South Africa and for many years to follow. Eventually I did become an expert and did not have to "act" the part any longer.

77

This new position meant a major move for us, from Johannesburg to the Eastern Transvaal, the so-called Lowveld. You reach those parts by driving some two-hundred miles east towards the Indian Ocean. About halfway there, you start to descend from the 6000 feet high plateau that forms most of the central parts of South Africa. The climate changes abruptly with the heat and humidity increasing dramatically, and soon you are in the little town of Nelspruit, the heart of the Lowveld.

My new employer provided a company car that I was allowed to use for personal trips. The car, a Pontiac station wagon the size of a small ship with suspension to match, suited our little family perfectly. Most of our essential and scant belongings fit into the back. The rest was shipped and arrived two weeks later with half of the stuff missing in transit. Not that it mattered all that much. I now received a decent salary and we would be able to afford the expense of replacing our old things. Right in the beginning that was a little hard though and we were going to need some credit— credit that was not available from the local bank. The assistant bank manager, who with sincere regrets gave me that verdict, suggested I visit the owner of the local grocery and hardware store, owned by an Indian by the name of Muggardjee. After forty years, I must admit, I am not sure if that is the correct spelling of the name of this kindest of gentlemen.

On broaching the subject of a little credit with him, after telling him that I worked for Kynoch, he immediately assured me, "Please sir you are not to worry about this matter at all. Get whatever you need to set up your lovely little family in your new home. Pay me back whenever is convenient. I will charge you no interest for six months and good luck in Nelspruit."

As easy as that and no wonder the man had the best and most prosperous store in town. We acquired whatever we needed from Mr. Muggardjee during the remainder of our stay in that area and paid back our initial debt within the agreed time. He actually became a good friend, as far as that was possible during those days of extreme apartheid, and always gave us fatherly advice and decent discounts on our purchases.

When we first arrived at Nelspruit, we had rented a little apartment in the nearby village of White River. The place was small and expensive and on asking Muggardjee if he knew of anything better, he suggested I look at a place he owned in the country, only five miles out of town. I could rent it for less than half of what I paid in White River and according to him, he had just recently renovated it completely. He gave me the key and directions and we all went to see it that same day.

It was situated at the end of a dirt road in the middle of some twenty acres of orange orchards that had been neglected, but could be revived to production level with a little love, hard work, fertilizer and pest control. Obviously, I was the right man for the job.

That same day I discussed it with my new landlord and offered to take care of the orchards in exchange for fifty percent of the profits—profits I knew I could wring out of those nice Valencia orange trees. We shook on it and did quite well out of those trees for the next couple of years.

Fredy and I were so happy with this new turn of events

that we bought and shared a bottle of excellent Cape wine, from Muggardjee of course, and celebrated the night of our moving in by making wild love on the kitchen floor. Don't ask me why on the floor while we had a perfectly good bed in the bedroom, but whatever the reason, the result was and still is my second son and love-child, Rudy, now a grown man with two beautiful sons of his own.

Perhaps I would be going a little too far if, for this, I also gave thanks to Mr. Muggardjee?

Rudy, the lovechild, with the rest of us

Chapter 10

CAMPING WITH ELEPHANTS

In one of the previous chapters, I mentioned the Van Meter Family. When I called on them for the first time in my position as a technical rep for a fertilizer manufacturer, I was received at the main homestead by a statuesque, dark-haired beauty, dressed in a large bath towel. As this was not exactly what I had anticipated, I initially only managed to stare at her and was then addressed with, "Well, can you speak, or should I bring you a piece of paper and a pencil?"

I then stuttered my introduction in Afrikaans (South African Dutch), upon which she interrupted me with the information that she did not speak the lingo and could I attempt to speak English, please. That I could and was then told that her husband and three sons were out hunting.

"You are welcome to go and look for them. They have gone north to the river and if you follow that road you might find them. But, let me warn you, they are a pretty trigger-happy bunch. Make sure you announce yourself clearly or you might get shot."

I decided to call on them some other time, and was

about to take my leave when a beat-up old Land Rover with a dead lion draped over the hood drove up in a cloud of dust.

"We got the bastard. He had just killed another one of our cows," announced the older man in the party. I introduced myself to Andree Van Meter and his three sons, David, Michael and Martin—all three in their early or mid-twenties—brandishing hunting rifles and wide smiles. As it was lunchtime, I was invited to share their meal, which was a good opportunity to get to know this clan a little better.

Sarah Van Meter, who was better known under her maiden name, Sarah Silver, was a former ballerina, turned ballet teacher in Johannesburg where she had her dance school and home. On realizing who she was, I told her that I had seen a recent performance of the group she was associated with.

"So, you are actually a civilized person and not like my family here. I am just visiting my sons and grandkids for a couple of days. Can't stand this wilderness and cultural desolation for much longer than that, and if it were not for our annual camping trip, I wouldn't be here just now."

This remark then prompted Andree to inform me that they all thanked the Lord that she was not on the farm all the time, as she would have driven them totally bonkers long ago. Whereupon David remarked, "Mom, we love you to death but, like alcohol, you need to be consumed in modest quantities."

Although David may have taken his own advice to heart in regard to his Mother, he did not seem to do so when it came to drinking beer, of which he and the others consumed large quantities to help wash down the delicious lamb chops and fried potatoes that were being served by a couple of rather fierce-looking Africans.

After this introduction to the Van Meters, I returned regularly and they became my friends and rather good customers. Their farming enterprises were extensive and successful. Apart from the very large cattle ranch, they owned several hundred acres of orange trees and grew hundreds of acres of cotton. They were well respected in the area and introduced me to a number of owners of neighboring farms, which was good for business. However, when I asked them to give me an intro to Buddy Marston, I was told, "Forget that bastard. We will not have anything to do with him."

Marston owned a large farm in the neighborhood and it now became clear that they were not on speaking terms. In fact, it was more like all-out war and according to the stories, shots had been exchanged on at least one occasion. The source of the dispute was labor, which was in short supply, particularly during the orange picking season. The Van Meters took very good care of their employees and Marston often struggled to get people to work for him.

They then explained that not so long ago, Marston, who owned and piloted his own crop spraying aircraft, had decided to buzz the Van Meter orchards while picking was in progress. The laborers, thinking they were being attacked with poison, scattered in all directions, spilling baskets of carefully picked fruit. Michael, who was supervising the work that day and was armed with a rifle for chasing away the rampaging herds of baboons, took a couple of pot-shots at Peter's plane, hitting it, although not critically. The lengthy court case that had followed ended in a stalemate. They were a wild and

83

trigger-happy bunch, indeed.

It was about a year after my first visit that they invited me to join the annual camping trip on the Limpopo River, which forms the border between South Africa and what was then Southern Rhodesia and now Zimbabwe. Although I realized that a vacation of that nature with the Van Meter clan could only end with a serious hangover, I could not resist. I had to experience this momentous affair that had been described to me by different sources as something close to a circus spectacle. Also, I was looking forward to meeting Sarah van Meter again.

What a circus it was! In the party were some thirty-five members of the clan, including guests and at least that number of African porters, cooks, maids and men servants to assist with camp preparation, cooking and hauling. Among all the goods transported to the shores of the mighty river, other than the usual camping gear, was a large generator to provide power for, among other things, three old refrigerators.

"No way are they going to be drinking warm beer," said Sarah.

There was also a large, old-fashioned bathtub, for those that were nervous about bathing in the crocodile-infested river that was also plagued by bilharzia, a disease, caused by blood-infecting parasitic flukes. The tub was equipped with its own pump and filter system, so that the water from the river could be purified. I'll never forget the sight of that tub, parked under an enormous baobab tree. Strangely enough, it did not look too much out of place with its brass lion's feet firmly planted in the African dirt and surrounded with a flimsy privacy screen that had been erected from mopani branches. Large, tent-like shades had been pitched to cover the camping tables that could comfortably seat the entire party in one sitting. All these efforts for a short and what was expected to become a very intense three-day vacation.

Soon after our arrival in the late afternoon, the cooks got busy preparing the charcoal grills to cook the evening meal, which would mainly consist of the game that the Van Meters had shot that same afternoon. There was going to be springbok and plenty of guinea fowl, to be served with lots of fresh veggies and sweet potatoes. For me, all this was very comforting, as I was a young man with tremendous appetites.

It was autumn and the weather was mild, with pleasant warm days and cool nights. That first night the evening meal was a rousing success with most everybody and that included the servants, eating and drinking more than they should have. A short skit performed by Sarah Silver-Van Meter and two of her Johannesburg colleagues followed the dinner. I can't recall the details of the little play, but vividly remember the mystical beauty of Sarah and her companions dancing by the firelight to the wild sounds of the drum circle, formed by five or six of the Africans. The dancers were soon joined by a number of the blacks, who turned the party into one of the few inter-racial events I would ever witness in that country, so horribly torn asunder by apartheid. I got into the dancing act myself and really let go. Let go, to the extent that to this day I cannot remember where or in whose tent I slept that night. Perhaps it was in the arms of an African beauty? I truly don't know, but would like to think so.

The next day was spent eating great meals, followed by

long siestas in the shade of the mighty Baobab trees. The more energetic among us went for hikes and/or hunting trips.

The remainder of our little safari should and would most likely have gone off without a hitch, had it not been for the drunken elephants! During late summer and autumn, the marula trees come to the end of their fruit-bearing season. It is then that its sweet fruit reach an overripe condition and start to ferment on the tree. Elephants love marulas and are known to overindulge at times, a little like most of the members of our party.

And so it happened that during the early evening of our second day, a couple of rowdy young bull elephants, whose anger at being shunned by the rest of the herd had been amplified by the effect of too much booze, stumbled on our campsite.

Big trouble for campers

And what havoc they caused! Tents were smashed, the bathtub stomped on, cars banged up, the refrigerators with our precious beer destroyed. It was a miracle that nobody was hurt. Fortunately, most were at the river at the time to watch the sundown, as otherwise there might have been a massacre. I was one of the few that had not joined the river party and therefore had the "pleasure" of witnessing the attack. It was a good thing that they clearly announced their arrival by loudly crashing through the almost impenetrable bush. On hearing them approach like a freight train on steroids, I ran like hell to one of the nearest trucks and jumped in, hoping they would not see me, or if they did, the good old Detroit steel would provide some protection.

Imagine my terror when one of them came straight at me, his enormous ears flapping and trunk curled up while his eyes glared malevolently, some five tons of muscle and bone ready to grind me, this puny invader of their domain, into the African dirt.

"Dust to dust," I spoke to myself, knowing I was done for, but at the very last moment, "Jumbo" swerved sideways and attacked and severely damaged one of the other cars. I swear that on passing he looked at me and rumbled, "Scared the crap out of you didn't I?"

Fortunately, they did not hang around too long. A little like a tornado, they blew through, did their utmost and continued on their way.

Soon the rest of the party returned. Most were very upset and angry at these wild animals for the destruction of their possessions and the untimely termination of the fabulous little vacation. Personally, I just sat there and thanked the Spirits for taking such good care of me. One of the Africans, who had also been present and had seen the elephant rushing at me, wanted to know, "Baas, what *Muti* (medicine) protected you from the *Indiovu* (the unstoppable one)? It must be very strong. Can the Baas please give me some?"

Africa, the way I knew and liked it, wild and wonderful.

Chapter 11

FRENCH FLYERS

Americans, and in fact most Anglos, have a tendency to look down their noses at the French. Anything French, other than French Fries, the Statue of Liberty and perhaps, Rousseau, is considered inferior. Admittedly, their performance against Hitler and his Nazis was not impressive. However, if Americans, like the French, had suffered 73.3% casualties during the First World War, we might have been a little gun-shy too. Yes, out of 8.4 million mobilized French, more than 6.1 million were killed, missing or wounded. That compares with American losses of 7.1 percent during that same conflict.

I do not want to bore you with statistics but, instead, will tell you about my experiences with a couple of Frenchmen who worked for me as helicopter pilots in South Africa.

We had been contracted to provide aerial pest control in cotton fields for a farmers' cooperative. Some 10,000 acres had to be treated weekly and, as the local geography did not allow the use of fixed wing aircraft, we used two Djinn turbo helicopters, manufactured in France. Tiny little two-seaters, very agile and maneuverable and perfectly suited to the job in hand. Jean and Marcel were veterans from the French Foreign Legion and, you guessed it, from Viet Nam where, before the USA, they also had a little run-in with the Viet Cong. Jean was about 6'4 and thin as a rake. Marcel was about half his height and seemingly, twice his weight. I admit to an occasional overstatement, but standing next to each other, they created that impression. Both, for very different reasons, barely fit into the little chopper seats. They were crack pilots, very good at their trade. A little dare-devilish at times and always looking for an opportunity to play a practical joke. The third member of the team was a full-time mechanic responsible for keeping the Djinns serviced and safe. He was a German by the name of Jochim, also a veteran of the Foreign Legion and, I suspect, the Luftwaffe. The pilots referred to him as "Le Bosch."

The French Djinn Helicopter in Action

For a German, Le Bosch fortunately had an unusually well developed sense of humor. He described Jean and Marcel as those "stubid kids that should have been spanked more often by their modders," and tolerated their antics with amazing magnanimity and patience. I sometimes wondered why he did not sabotage their machines.

Jochim drove a nice old Mercedes, which like the Djins, he kept clean as a whistle and in perfect condition. The "stubid kids" would continuously mess around with his car. In one instance, while poor Jochim was working on their choppers and his car was parked in some tall grass, they put blocks under the rear axle so that the wheels were just touching but not enough to get traction. Then they sat back to watch the show, but only after taking elaborate leave of Jochim and warning him not to drive too fast.

Jochim's, "Verdamt nochmals, next time I vill keel dees stubid kids," solicited much laughter, followed by the two Frenchmen removing the blocks and presenting "Le Bosch" with a nice bottle of wine.

Now that we are on that subject, let me just assure you that what they say about the French and their proclivity for wine consumption was clearly substantiated by these two gallant representatives of La Douce France. In fact, my close association with them for that one season nearly turned me into a perfect model for that part of French culture. I have ever since been imbibing modest, but regular quantities of red wine, and that of course, very much to the benefit to my general health.

My role in this little operation was coordination and collection. I had to decide which fields needed to be treated and when, and then to collect payment for the services rendered. We all worked very hard, in particular the pilots, as the choppers were in the air for five to six days a week, for as much as ten hours per day. At the end of the week, we returned to a base camp at a small local airport. I was often delivered to my home by helicopter and picked up again early on Monday mornings. Yes, our lawn was not only frequented by high reaching giraffes, but at times also by low flying machines.

photo by Joseph Gill www.worldglobetrotters.cm

Watch out for the flying machines

These trips, specifically with the roly-poly Marcel at the controls were at times, to say the least, enervating. He enjoyed hopping power lines by flying only a few feet above the ground until it seemed it would be too late to pull up-and-over. However, he always did and then looked at me to see how I was "enjoying" the fun. It was a good thing I was somewhat of a thrill seeker.

It was on one of our trips back to the airport that I had an opportunity to witness what these two young men really were capable of. Until that time, their mostly juvenile pranks had been amusing, but nothing in their behavior had signaled a resolute willingness to risk limb and life for the benefit of others.

As we were flying in formation along a deserted country road that would lead us back to the airport, we overtook a lone car traveling at high speed, leaving a trail of ochre dust. Just as we were approximately overhead, at an altitude of about 500 feet, the car swerved wildly — probably the result of a blown tire. Although the driver attempted to keep the vehicle on the road, it soon spun out of control, and rolled over several times, before coming to a stop on its roof in a cloud of dust.

In a maneuver that they must have learned and practiced during their air force training, and which they executed without prior radio consultation, the choppers peeled away from each other while in steep descent, to come to almost simultaneous landings some fifty feet on either side of the vehicle.

It was just at that moment flames were beginning to come from the front end of the car. Jean and Marcel, both armed with fire extinguishers from their craft, were dousing the flames within thirty seconds of our landing. We heard muffled screams from within the car and as the blaze seemed to be under control, Jean handed me his extinguisher while he and Marcel both tackled the doors. At any moment the fire could reignite with the real possibility of a serious explosion. One door was wrenched open and Jean crawled half inside to soon come out with a boy of some ten years old. After handing the child to Marcel, he dived in again to emerge once more with what later proved to be the mother. She was unconscious, appeared to have a broken leg and was bleeding badly from a head wound. The boy had scrapes and scratches, but otherwise seemed to be in reasonable shape, just screaming for his mother to be saved.

The first aid kits were pulled out, the woman's leg stabilized and her head wound bandaged. She was then strapped into the passenger seat of Marcel's chopper while I took the boy on my lap in Jean's machine. In less than thirty minutes after the accident, we were air-born again and on our way to the nearest hospital, some forty miles away. While in the air, Jean radioed the airport with instruction to inform the hospital of our imminent arrival. Twenty-five minutes later, we touched down on a spacious lawn in front of the hospital where doctors and nurses immediately took over. "Mission completed!"

A mother and her son had been saved from almost certain death by the unselfish, resolute actions of these two young Frenchmen. Both were awarded medals, but what seemed to please them more were the profuse expressions of thanks from the mother, who recuperated completely. She and her husband invited us all for a major cook-out and party on their farm, where the entire community showed up and the medals were pinned to Jean's and Marcel's chests.

Marcel, on being asked what he would do with his medal, responded with a nonchalant, "I suppose I'll put it in the box with the others."

Chapter 12

FLYING A FORD FAIRLANE

After drinking a couple of bottles of red wine—a couple of bottles each—with my two buddies Marcel and Jean, the French helicopter pilots, I climbed into my brand-new, 1964 Ford Fairlane with the idea of driving some ninety miles to go home and to bed. That did not quite happen as planned.

This beauty was one of the first Ford compacts. As the American public was looking for economy in name and appearance only—what else is new—these cars all came with V8 engines and all the luxury options one could imagine. A little like the Studebaker Larks of similar size that came out a couple of years earlier. My Fairlane 500, or let me be more precise, the company's Fairlane 500, came with a 289 hp engine, a stick shift and leather upholstery. It was white with a bright red stripe along its flanks and could go like lightning. For some reason, that escapes me now, my kids referred to it as the fire engine. It was a sturdy little gas-guzzler with a lovely and loud, basso rumble that could be heard for miles, particularly after I had removed the mufflers. My customers, depending on weather they were in need of my services or not, would either run for the hills on my approach or, as I would like to think, stand ready with their checkbooks to place their orders. Believe it or not, but I did not do too badly in that respect.

The much abused Ford Fairlane

I remember distinctly, when I seated myself comfortably behind the steering wheel of my beloved Fairlane, that my friends entreated me in their best Charles Chevalier English, "Pleese Erman, you ave been drinking, not too much of course, but more than is good for driving this fast car. Peraps you should let us fly you ome in the elicopter. Yes?"

"In your condition, you boys couldn't fly a kite, let alone a turbo-jet helicopter. Besides, you have to go to sleep now and dream of your sisters, as you French are wont to do!" With that said I floored the gas and skidded temporarily out of trouble in a cloud of leaded exhaust fumes.

My way home took me for some sixty miles on a brand-new blacktopped road that for the first fifty miles was straight as a dye, without even the slightest curve. Also, at that time of the night there was no traffic and from experience I knew that I was not likely to encounter anyone at all. The road took me through a peaceful and sparsely populated native reserve with here and there a small kraal. The people that lived there subsisted on beef and goat production.

The brand-new road leading through all that emptiness offered the perfect opportunity to test this car's mettle. Could it really do one hundred miles an hour as advertised? I was determined to find out and was cruising along comfortably with the speedometer at 80 when I decided that now was the time to see what it could really do. With the pedal to the floor, the speedometer needle gradually kept creeping up, first to 90 then 95 and eventually to a glorious 100 miles per hour. I know for sure as I clearly remember the needle hitting the mark. On returning my eyes to the road, I also remember, even more clearly, seeing a lot of cattle sleeping on the pavement. The nights were cool and these animals, unaware as they were of my foolishness, had been seeking the warmth of the sun-heated tarmac.

I did apply the brakes but by far too late. This was before the era of disc brakes and these had not been designed to slow down a couple tons of steel from hell-for-leather to full-stop. My poor, brand-new, lovely Fairlane with its pleasant growl hit the first couple of cows in the road and went airborne. I distinctly remember the short and eerie peace of flight. It was followed by total mayhem of which I was barely conscious. I braced myself as well as I could and reflexively held on to the steering wheel with all my might. This car was the first I ever drove that came equipped with front seat lap-belts and luckily I had it strapped tight. I had been taught to use them while flying around with the two Frenchmen in their choppers. Later it became clear that the car had rolled over several times to "safely" land on its wheels, some fifty feet away from the road.

As soon as it came to a stop, I got out and realized that I was more or less OK. I had a cut over my eye that bled like hell and a dislocated thumb that I absentmindedly relocated to its proper position. The only sounds I detected were a gentle hissing, produced by the car's leaking radiator and the anguished moaning from one of the cows I had hit. After an initial, "Serves you right for lying in the middle of the road," I soon felt sorry for the suffering animal and dispatched it with the revolver I always carried on these trips.

Well, what next? It would be daylight before I could expect to be found and after the Fairlane's engine had cooled off some and the danger of fire had passed, I decided to make myself comfortable in the luxury of its leather interior.

I must have dozed off a little, when I heard some voices. Apart from the revolver, the cubbyhole also contained a flashlight and sure enough, it soon found the source of these voices. Three Africans armed with knobkerries—a type of fighting stick with a good-sized knob on one end, to be used for bashing in heads—came hesitantly in my direction. I immediately warned them that I was armed and asked them what they wanted.

"Hauk, Baas we hear accident and want to help. We also see the dead animals and that no good. They are my animals and who will pay for dead cows?"

I knew this was not going to be easy unless I could satisfy them that they would be paid. I started by telling them however that it was their own fault as they should not allow the cows to sleep on the road.

Upon which the speaker came back with, "You build big road through our lands, you should build fence also. Baas, cows not very expensive and you are rich and can pay. Only twenty rand, each."

Twenty rand in those days was a lot of money and after a little haggling we agreed on thirty rand for both animals. Fortunately I had collected a cash payment from one of my customers that day and I paid them then and there. From that instant on they were all friendly and helpful and wanted to know what I intended to do with my recently acquired dead cows.

Well, what does one do with dead cows, when one is young and hungry?

"My friends," I said, "What about I give you back the cows, or at least most of them, provided you cook us up a feast of fresh steaks and some corn?"

"OK, baas, we also hungry. We come back quick and cut some steaks and make 'groot braai'. Wait here please."

For those of you uninitiated in the South African lingo, 'Braai' is a cook-out and groot braai is monster cook-out. And it wasn't long before they were back. This time the group had grown to some twenty men and women, all ready for a free meal and some fun. They loaded the dead animals on a cart drawn by a donkey and invited me to follow. When I showed a little uncertainty about leaving the Fairlane, the trunk of which was loaded with very costly helicopter parts, they assured me not to worry and instructed a couple of the pickaninnies to watch the "motor."

The kraal, where they all seemed to live, was just a couple hundred yards away — sort of hidden behind a number of large trees. There were at least a dozen mud and concrete block huts with thatch roofs surrounding a central community area with a well, next to which some of the women were busy building a fire in a large fire pit.

Someone produced an old wicker chair and invited me to sit down and make myself comfortable. I must admit to having felt rather insecure and out of place, and for a while considered just sneaking off to the car to wait there for an early-morning ride to town. However, by now it was just one in the morning and I knew I would not be able to sleep for fear of being attacked while sitting out there on my own. I decided to stick around and enjoy the show. From this position I could see what was happening and I did get some confidence from having the enforcer stuck under my belt.

The smaller one of "my cows," the one I had had to shoot, had been hung from a tree by its hind legs and was being skinned within minutes after our arrival at the kraal. One of the women came over and said, "I am Anna. Perhaps Baas is thirsty and like to drink Coca Cola?"

On answering in the affirmative she left and soon returned with a couple of bottles of the stuff — not exactly ice cold but cool and drinkable. This was going to be better than I expected, perhaps?

The fellow who had done the talking during the negotiations over the sale of the animals appeared to be the head man of the village—giving orders in an authoritarian tone—orders that were promptly followed by the others. I realized now that he was an older person, graying at the temples and limping slightly. After the first steaks had been cut, he walked over and while the meat was being cooked over a makeshift grill, engaged me in conversation.

In excellent English he admonished me, "Baas is young and sometimes young men do things that are not good for them. Sorry for speaking like that and Baas will forgive me, but driving so fast through this area can be dangerous. You was lucky for living after the crash and you was also lucky for me, Jimson, being here to protect you. Some of these men were going to beat you for killing the oxen. Perhaps they would have killed you."

While he was giving me this little speech I looked at him closely and the fire light disclosed what I thought was a somewhat sardonic, but humorous, glint in his eyes. With that as an indication that a little sparring was in order, I said, "Jimson, you are a kind and wise man and I thank you for your words of warning. Don't you think that these men, the ones that were going to beat me, do not know as well as you do, that the police would immediately suspect the people from your kraal? And Jimson, you know what the police in this country will do to get confessions. It would not be enough to say "I didn't do it." They would beat you real bad and then throw you all in jail."

Jimson didn't have to think long about that and said, "Ja, Baas, that what you say about the polisi is right, but we blacks sometime are very hot-blooded and angry, angry with white men and what they do to us and then we sometimes forget to think about what can happen later."

By now some of the meat had apparently been cooked. The same young woman that had brought me the Cokes now came over with an enormous platter of steaks that smelled delicious. Both Jimson and I helped ourselves and without much formality, other than an "Eet smaaklik" (bon appétit), we attacked the meat with eager gusto, glad for an excuse to end this discussion. It was also a good thing that just after the subject of murder had come up, the fire was not bright enough to throw much light on our rather gruesome and bloody meal. Bloody, as the steaks were *done* very rare. In fact, while I was eating I realized they were just barely warm and wondered if that was the result of lingering body heat of the recently expired animal or the result of holding them over the fire for a bit.

After quickly devouring our first steaks, Jimson suggested, "Baas is young and can eat much." With that he called for more meat and some corn porridge, "Anna, breng meer vleis en mielie pap en cook the meat better."

We all, and that includes the whole village, ate well that night. After Jimson and I had eaten our fill, we sat there peacefully smoking cigarettes. We exchanging few words that were interrupted with long periods of satisfying silence and an occasional loud burp.

It was not long until sun-up. A passing motorist gave me a ride to town. Looking at the *juicy* blood stains on my shirt he wanted to know if the "kaffirs" had beaten me up.

Chapter 13

A DIFFERENT TWIST TO GAME PRESERVATION

As a result of my destruction of a perfectly good Ford Fairlane, my employer came to the conclusion that fast cars were not good for me and replaced the Fairlane with, of all makes, a Peugeot 404, a perfectly nice little car, but no speedster. It's not just speed that can cause accidents however.

At that time we lived only some ten miles from the Kruger Wildlife Park. As there were no fences around the park, and the wild animals did not know where the park ended and the farms began, there were a lot of them roaming free in that part of the country. At times, when the wind was out of the east one could hear the lions roar, very much to the dismay of my bull terriers who on those occasions would rush out into the bush, ready to tackle the invaders. More brawn than brains and fortunately the lions never came that close.

I now have two standard poodles, and I imagine that were they ever to hear lions roar, they would more likely jump into bed with me than rush out to protect the homestead. But then, poodles are reported to be the most intelligent of all breeds. Who needs brawn if you have smarts?

If I had had a little more smarts, I might not have landed in trouble during one of my sales calls to Hendrik Prinsloo, a cattle farmer some sixty miles from my home. I happened to arrive on his birthday, which was in the process of being celebrated with lots of beer and a major 'Braai'. Always game for a party, it took little convincing to get me to join the festivities. This would in any case have been the last call of the day and a couple of beers were not going to hamper my ability to find my way home.

Parties had a way of interfering with my life and this one was no exception. The talk around the fire was about a cheetah that had been sighted in the area—another unwelcome stray from the Kruger park. It had already killed several young heifers that belonged to farmers in the area and plans were made to hunt him down during the coming days. Little did I suspect that I would be passively involved!

My intentions to leave after a couple of beers did not come to fruition. Truth is that a couple of beers soon became half a dozen and by the time I got into my nice little Peugeot, I was in no condition to drive. By that time, it was past ten o'clock, but before he let me go, Hendrik insisted I take a large bag of fresh, raw sirloin steaks, which he deposited on the back seat of my car.

The roads in that part of the country were mostly poorly maintained dirt roads, without signposts or directions of any nature. As I was more than a little under the weather and still unfamiliar with that particular section of my territory, I was soon very lost. Had I been inclined to ask for directions, and as you know most men are not, there would have been no one to ask.

I must have been driving around in circles, as after a couple of hours I was very tired but nowhere near my destination and, as I found out later, only a few miles from my point of departure. So extremely tired, that my system decided to take a little time off. However, with my foot still on the accelerator the Peugeot kept moving along at some fifty miles per hour.

When I woke up from my little snooze, I was parked on a big rock, wedged in between two rather hefty hardwood trees, some distance away from the road. As this happened in the pre-seatbelt and airbag era, I must have been under the watchful eye of that certain angel that protects drunks and fools. Other than a gusher of a nosebleed and a rather sore knee, there were no apparent ill effects to my physique. The Peugeot had not done so well. The engine ran and the rear wheels merrily turned, but that to little avail, as they were some six inches off the ground. This was due to the fact that the entire car sat teetering on top of a big old rock.

Well, it was time to start walking. A little fresh air would not be harmful. I found myself some 100 feet from the road and had to climb a steep embankment to get back to it. No easy task that was, with my throbbing knee. Once there I did at first not have a clue which direction to take, but being an avid sailor, I knew a little about celestial navigation. The sky was clear, and in the southern hemisphere, the Milky Way stands out like a wide streak of light across the heavens. With the help of the Milky Way and the Southern Cross, I figured out the general direction and started limping along, hoping against all odds that someone might drive by and give me a ride.

Again my guardian angel came to my rescue, as soon, a rickety bus packed with African laborers on their way to work stopped and after questioning me, gave me a ride to a cross road not far from my home. The driver wanted to know what I was doing there that early in the morning.

"Did the wild animals attack the young Basie?" he asked mockingly.

Basie is the diminutive for Baas and I was a little offended. I must have been quite a sight with the blood from my broken nose all over my clothes, and as they were all laughing gleefully, I appeared to be providing some comic relief for these early morning travelers. At least that part was positive, although I did not quite see it that way at the time. I may have been young, but at six foot three, certainly not little.

Anyway, thanks to them I did make it home by sunrise, just in time to be received by the young man who worked for us in the house, with the remark, "Hauk, poor Basie, was you attacked by the animals?"

My wife's observations were somewhat less compassionate, "Were you drunk again you bloody fool? One of these days you are going to kill yourself and then, what will I and the children do?"

As she was plainly stating the facts and there was no point in arguing reality, I had a cold shower and went to sleep. On waking up a couple hours later, I called a friend who owned a tow-truck and asked him to give me a hand retrieving my poor vehicle. I thought I remembered more or less where I had left it, but it took us several hours of driving around before we finally located it. Had it not been silver-grey with the sunlight reflecting off it, we might never have found it. There it sat, high and dry on its rock, but hidden between the Mopani trees. It was impossible to get within fifty feet with the tow truck, but the cable on the winch plus an extension was long enough to reach it.

On approaching, I noticed a strange noise coming from within the car and on peering through the rear window, I realized we had a visitor. Were the jokes about the wild animals attacking me about to come true?

Spread out on the rear seat was a full-grown cheetah. The doors were closed and he could not get out. On leaving, I must have left one of the doors open, and attracted by the gift of my host of the previous evening—about ten pounds of lovely raw beefsteak—the cheetah had jumped inside for a ready meal. No killing required. His weight must have jolted the car sufficiently to close the door behind him.

Not on my backseat please

He was trapped, but in a way, so were we. I was not about to open the door to let him out and have him finish his dinner with me as the main course. Fortunately, he did get enough air as some of the windows were partially open.

We stopped at the home of one of the local farmers. A couple of calls brought the park rangers out that same afternoon. They tranquilized the cheetah, captured him alive and later released my "dinner guest" in the Game Park. In the end, this little escapade probably saved his life. He had strayed too far from his home and sooner or later would have been shot by one of the local ranchers. I called Hendrik and told him I had taken care of his cheetah problem. I was rewarded with some more steaks, which this time, I got to eat myself.

Although my nose was set expertly, I managed to put my boss's nose severely out of joint with that little escapade. My next company car was a hand-me-down from the car pool.

Chapter 14

SUNDAY MORNING VISIT

Like most young people, my wife and I were usually tardy in getting up in the mornings and on Sundays, we slept as long as the children would let us. They were pretty good at that and it was therefore really surprising that on this Sunday someone was crying like a baby and woke us up. I looked at my watch. Our youngest was not a baby anymore and at six-thirty probably asleep.

I turned on my back to be able to look around our spacious bedroom. It was full daylight and the windows to the screened porch were wide open, and to allow free flow of air, so were the curtains. Again we heard the strange little baby cry and just at that moment I noticed some movement of the curtain. Two little eyes were peering at me from the top of the curtain rail. They stared at me steadily and now I realized I was looking into the eyes of a Lesser Bush Baby, known in Afrikaans as Nagapie.

My wife had also woken up and both of us remained quietly on our backs watching the show. I soon realized our little visitor was carrying a baby and as everything must have appeared peaceful to her, she started to descend from her perch, climbing down the curtain until she reached the floor, where she now disappeared from our field of vision behind the foot of our bed. Wondering what would be her next move, we stayed as still as we could and just as I was getting ready to sit up and see where our visitor had disappeared to, she leaped from the floor and landed securely on the bed between my legs. At not more than eight inches and perhaps ten ounces, her landing made not much of an impact.

Again, there was a stalemate. None of us stirred for about a minute or two and it was our guest that made the next move. She quietly advanced onto my stomach and after reaching my chest, not ten inches from my face, she sort of handed me her baby. Leaving this little worm that can't have put more than two ounces on the scale, she then slowly retreated a little, presumably to see how I would deal with her child. I picked up the tiny creature, this Bush Baby baby and put it into the pocket of my pajama jacket, from which it peaked out at Mom.

I must have measured up to the mother's expectations, as now she turned around and in a few amazing leaps left the room, leaving us in charge of her offspring. My wife and I looked at each other in dumbfounded amazement. In a way this was one of the most touching things that had ever happened to me. Here I was this big ape of a hundred and ninety pounds, suddenly entrusted with the care of a baby of the smallest of all primates—by nobody less than its own mother? What could possibly have motivated this wild little creature to abandon her child? Was she going to have a last fling before settling down or was her usual abode threatened by some lurking danger? We never quite figured that out, but knew for sure that she must have had a much higher regard for my capabilities as a parent than the evidence could support.

In the meantime our kids were up and the whole family gathered on the bed. My daughter, Martine, who loved all living creatures and was always taking care of some really unusual pets—she even had a praying mantis that she carried around with her wherever she went, even to school—was put in charge of feeding Bigeyes. That's what she named him as soon as she saw him. We agreed that her carnivorous praying mantis would have to share the bugs, Martine caught for him, with our new guest. With that decision taken, I attempted to hand over Bigeyes to my daughter, but Bigeyes wasn't having any of that. He must have been instructed by his mother to stick with me and that is what he was determined to do. He held onto me for dear life and for fear of hurting him, we agreed that he might as well stay with me for the time being. Because of his obstinate stubbornness and refusal to be handled by anyone other than myself, my wife and daughter had determined that Bigeyes must be a boy.

For the next three days this little guy stuck to me like glue, riding around in my shirt pocket, eating little bugs and tiny crumbs of bread and drinking honeyed water from a miniature bottle Martine used for feeding baby mice. One of the positive side effects of carrying a baby around in your shirt pocket is the inability to place a pack of cigarettes in that same receptacle. Try it—you will smoke less, as I did.

Herman Thorbecke

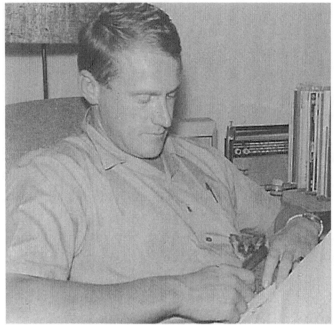
Bigeyes

Bush babies, like most lemurs, are nocturnal animals, active at night and at rest during the daytime. Bigeyes, true to his origins, slept most of the day in his pouch and at night came to life. As that was a bit of a problem for me, the babysitter, I fashioned a little cage in which we kept him during the few hours he let me sleep. We had found out that nocturnal animals do not make the best pets, unless you are a night owl yourself.

It was therefore a good thing that on the evening of his third day with us, Mom suddenly reappeared just as we were ready to turn off the light. She entered as she had before, through the window and jumped on the bed. Bigeyes had not been placed in his cage yet and she eagerly accepted him as

112

soon as I handed him over.

She didn't stay around to say thank you, but in a way her faith and trust in us took ample care of that. We felt well rewarded and fully gratified for our services as Bush Baby baby-sitters.

Herman Thorbecke

Chapter 15

IMMORAL RELATIONS

My friend and colleague, Peter Phillips, told me most of the following story, about Callie Du Plessis and Jamie Van Heerden. Peter, Jamie and I were employed by the same corporation and while they lived in Johannesburg, I was stationed in the Northern Transvaal. I have only added some details to fill in the backgroud and inform readers, that may not be familiar with nineteen-sixties South Africa.

Callie Du Plessis was a "Cape Colored," a mixed blood descendant from Africans and/or Malays and Europeans. She was a typical representative of her race, a slender, olive-skinned beauty with a fabulous head of dark curls. During the apartheid years, her ancestry was the least desirable. Coloreds were neither here nor there, and treated by both whites and blacks as inferior and impure, like bastards. Malays were considered outsiders that had been brought to the Cape by the Dutch, as a reliable and easily subdued labor force during the seventeenth and eighteenth centuries.

She was a stage actress and a colleague of Naomi Silk, an actress herself and Peter's upstairs neighbor and close

115

friend. Both women were working for a well-known Johannesburg theatre group and were socially involved, as far as that was possible, within the choking restraints of the apartheid laws and regulations. Peter had seen Callie in some of Naomi's plays. Her roles were limited to those she would normally have played in real life, that of a maid servant, farm worker, or other position of a subservient nature. She was an amazing actress, strikingly beautiful and always a presence, both on and off the stage. She also had a great voice and in his opinion was wasting her time in South Africa.

As mentioned, Naomi lived in the penthouse apartment above his more modest abode and loved to throw an occasional wild party. That is how they met. One evening, shortly after he had moved into the building, one of these rather loud events kept him from sleeping.

From here on, I will let Peter relate the story in his own words.

Ready to tell *"these people"* their fortune, I went upstairs, knocked on the door and was invited in by Callie. Presuming she was the maid, I asked her to please tell the Missus that I would like to speak to her.

She looked me over, smiled sweetly and replied, "I am the Missus, what can I do for you young man?" This so totally took me by surprise that all I managed to utter were some idiotic mumblings about the noise.

"Well, can you try to be a little more explicit, or shall I call the maid, so you can explain yourself to her?" She then turned around and shouted, "Naomi, there is some chap to see you. Shall I let him in?"

"Sure, if you like him!"

Well, in spite of my very stupid behavior, Callie seemed to approve of me, because she grabbed me by the arm and dragged me inside.

After that first occasion, I became a regular guest at Naomi's place and was introduced to a section of the South African public, the existence of which I might have suspected but would never have become acquainted with, had it not been for these two amazing women. Naomi's friends were from various walks of life, but all had one thing in common — they were very much opposed to the current regime and hated apartheid. Other than Callie, there were a small number of coloreds and blacks in the group.

Racially mixed gatherings like Naomi's parties, as you well know, are illegal and actually require a permit. Although politics were often discussed, these were not political meetings, but innocent gatherings of good friends. However, there was always the risk of someone denouncing her to the police, and in the event of a raid during one of her mixed gatherings, the consequences would have been very unpleasant. I believed she was playing a dangerous game, and just by attending, so was I.

Were I to be caught at one of her shindigs, my visitor's work permit (Peter was a Brit) might have been revoked and I deported. Well, to be honest, I like the excitement. I also strongly believe that I should have the right to pick my friends where I find them.

One of these friends was our colleague, Dr. Jamie Van Heerden, a biologist, in charge of a research project that our company had underway. You know him, Herman, he is the Afrikaner that used to play for the Springboks. A nice chap, open minded and liberal, but like most South Africans, he never quite considered Africans to be his equals. Shameful arrogance, you say and rightly so, but hard to evade for people who grew up in South Africa.

I do not know what made me do this, but on a whim I invited him to one of Naomi's parties. I suppose I was curious to see how he would deal with the black guests that would, as usual, be there. Jamie was in his early thirties, single, tall and good looking. He used to play full back for the Stellenbosch University rugby team and until he was injured, for the national team, the Springboks. In that role he is still well known, a sort of national hero. When I told Naomi I would like to bring him along to her upcoming birthday party, she was actually excited to get an opportunity to meet this famous rugby player and said, "Just make sure he is aware that there will be a mixed crowd!"

Jamie had no problems with meeting a mixed crowd. "I don't have a problem with that; I was practically brought up by my nanny. I know these people very well!" Yeah right. I had to remind him that these blacks were not exactly like his nannies and garden boys.

On the evening of the party, we met at my apartment, had a couple of beers and trekked upstairs. There Naomi received us graciously, with compliments on Jamie's rugby career, telling him what a stud he was. Linking her arm through his, she then proceeded to introduce him to her other guests.

Jamie seemed to be totally at ease, chatting and joking effortlessly with everyone. His trips overseas, playing rugby in France, England and Australia, had taken some of the rough edges off this farmer's son. Speaking English with his thick Afrikaans accent, I heard him exchange friendly barbs with a black college professor, who jokingly claimed that were they to permit blacks to play in the all white Springboks rugby team, Jamie would have been the only white player good enough to make the cut.

One of the last guests he was introduced to, was Callie. Suddenly, Jamie visibly lost his composure and after stammering a couple of polite remarks, attempted to excuse himself. "I really enjoyed talking to you, Ms. Callie, but let me go and refresh my drink and then I will perhaps see you a little later."

However, Callie was not quite done with him yet and said, "Oh, don't be so formal, *Master van Heerden*. Callie will do just fine; we are all friends here. Let me show you where you can find another beer." Holding him by his arm, she then steered him into the direction of the kitchen and out of range of my immediate attention. It was a sight to see though—this little colored girl taking command of the big white man, as if she were used to commanding them around on a regular basis. And as you well know, in South Africa, at this time in history, that was a most unusual spectacle.

As I had my own diversion, in the person of a visiting Brittish actress, I sort of lost track of Jamie for several hours until Naomi remarked, "Those two young kids from Stellenbosch seem to be hitting it off pretty well. They have been sitting on the roof garden for several hours, practically holding hands!"

I told Naomi to stop exaggerating and being such a romantic. There was no way square Dr. James van Heerden

119

was going to fall for Callie. Other than it being against the law, it was also against all the principles of his Afrikaner people and their religious beliefs. I decided to go and investigate all the same and found them, if not actually holding hands, certainly very close and in deep conversation. They were sitting opposite of each other, at a patio table, with their hands almost touching on the tabletop. When they heard me approach, he hurriedly sat back. Callie, however, just looked up and said, "Peter, I like your rugby player, he is different. Make him visit us again please." All Jamie did was laugh a little nervously, while he blushed like a schoolboy.

We sat around some more, and as it was getting very late and Jamie was more than just a little under the influence, we decided to retreat to my place. He wisely agreed to accept my offer to overnight on the couch. During breakfast he assured me that he had enjoyed the party tremendously and confided that Callie had asked him to come and see her current play. Could I make the arrangements, and we would then go together? My protestations that I had already seen the play were countered with the assertion that seeing it a second time would not do me any harm. Also, he did not feel comfortable going alone. Perhaps he felt he needed to be chaperoned?

A couple of weeks later we went to see the play. Every time Callie, who acted in one of her comical maidservant roles, came on the stage, poor Jamie's face glowed with admiration while he laughed louder than anyone else in the theatre. It was pretty clear that he was smitten badly, and I was a little concerned. After the performance we were invited backstage, where in accordance with the strict apartheid laws, we could only enter the dressing rooms of the white actors. Naomi assured Jamie not to worry. He would see Callie later at her apartment, as we were both invited for drinks and a midnight supper. The three of us would go together, and Callie and some others would come over on their own steam.

There was only a small group, and after a supper of asparagus, prosciutto and really good champagne, we all ended up dancing by candle light to music that seemed to slow down as the night progressed. I do not remember too much of that evening, but can still see Jamie and Callie clinging to each other as if their lives depended on it.

Sometime during the early morning hours I must have gone home and to bed. Waking up later that day, I was curious how the evening had ended for everyone and called Naomi on the phone. She told me that "the young couple" had not yet emerged from her spare bedroom. She thought it was a big joke, but I knew there was need for some urgent damage control and asked Naomi to make sure they left separately and to tell Jamie to come by my place on the way out.

A little later, he showed up and admitted sheepishly that this whole thing was sort of out of his control. I told him to stop thinking with his dick and that he should understand that this could only be a onetime fling, unless he had no objection to spending six months in jail. Never mind what that would do for his career. As a South African, he was very aware of the consequences and in fact told me about a good friend of his who had suffered exactly the fate I had described. Fired from his job and shunned by friends and even his family, the fellow had blown his brains out with a shotgun. I believed him, as there were almost daily stories in the press

121

about similar tragedies.

On that note we parted that day, I thinking that he had probably come to his senses. I felt very sorry for Callie, who according to Naomi had fallen deeply for James and kept asking Naomi to invite him to her next party.

It never came to that however. About three months later they were both arrested in Jamie's apartment. They were charged under the *Immorality Act* for having "sexual relations with a member of another race." Seamy language to match the sordid laws.

I heard all this from his attorney, who called me with a request to appear as a character witness at the preliminary hearing. Apparently, Jamie had contacted Callie at the theatre and after a brief rendezvous following one of her performances, she had agreed to meet at his place. They might have gotten away with that once or twice, but it became a regular thing. Other occupants of the building must have noticed and someone informed the police. They were caught, *in flagrante delicto*.

The rest of the events had been known to me for some time. The day following the arrest, the whole story had been all over the newspapers: "Famous Rugby Star Arrested under the Immorality Act for Having Sex with Colored Actress." This was followed by lots of ugly detail and mean-spirited conjecture about the actress probably luring the upstanding young Afrikaner into an *immoral relationship*.

He was bailed out of prison, and was told to come to work as if nothing had happened. Naomi attempted to do the same for Callie, but this game was not played on an even playing field. She was considered a risk, and bail was denied. There was nothing anyone could do and had Naomi not threatened to quit, right in the middle of the current season, her employers would have fired Callie on the spot.

Apartheid laws did not allow for a joined court case; God forbid that blacks would appear on an equal footing with white people. Their cases were held separately and as top lawyers defended both they would probably have gotten away with short sentences. However, Jamie decided to turn his day in court into an opportunity to accuse his government of the cruel suppression of his basic human right to choose a partner. Having his say cost him four months in prison, while Callie received the maximum sentence of six months.

Their affair received national and international attention, in a way that later worked in their favor. As soon as Callie came out of prison, she and Jamie applied for exit visas, which were promptly denied. They wanted each other and were determined to be together legally. That could only become reality outside the borders of South Africa. They stayed in touch but were more careful this time, awaiting an opportunity to leave. The possibility of slipping over the border was discussed and seriously considered. However, when the theatre company announced it was going on tour in England and Europe, there was no need for clandestine moves of that nature. The company had enough clout to get Callie an exit visa.

Shortly thereafter, Jamie applied for a post in Australia, which he had seen advertised by another Swiss conglomerate. They invited him for an interview in Switzerland, and this time with that written invitation in hand he did get a permit to leave. By the time he arrived there, Callie was already on tour in Europe. They were married in London. Jamie was offered the job in Australia, and last I heard, they still live there and have a large family.

Peter's account of the affair had ended with the admission that he himself almost fell for Callie's charms, but that she had not fallen for his.

In the meantime, even in South Africa and thanks mainly to Mandela, most now know that integration can work.

Chapter 16

PLAY CRICKET

I don't know a thing about cricket, or baseball for that matter. I have noticed there are similarities, and one of them is that the supporters in the stands have a tendency to consume more beer than is needed to quench their thirst. It is my theory that this is so, because watching either of these seemingly endless games while stone sober, is practically impossible.

So why did I agree to join my friends on a trip to watch a "Test Match" between the Australian and South African national teams? Don't ask me as I am now at a total loss to give you a solution to that riddle. All I can tell you is that I lived to regret making that decision!

This little adventure ran its course in sixties. I was a technical rep for a chemicals manufacturer and the friends that invited me were farmers and customers. There were four of us going on this fateful trip. Apart from myself, there were Frans Van der Merwe, David Herschfeld and Angus O'Flaherty. A sort of motley and diverse crew. Frans being a real Afrikaner, David a Jew, Angus an Irishman and the writer a Dutchman. "Did you hear the one about the Irishman, the

Jew and..."

The match was to be played in Johannesburg and we would fly there. Frans Van der Merwe was a veteran of the South African Air Force and the owner of a four seat Cessna aircraft. I was told he was an excellent pilot and with his background in jet fighters, I had no reason to doubt that. David was also a pilot and had just recently obtained his single engine license. Angus and I would be in good hands with the two of them flying the plane. Angus claimed that if it came to the push he could also pilot one of these things, but presumably not from the backseat.

Our Irish friend was a bit of a character. Apart from being a great farmer he was also an outstanding alcoholic, who was at all times intoxicated but never drunk. I remember talking business with him in his farm office while one of the farm hands was washing the windows from the outside. At least that is what he was supposed to be doing. The man appeared to be high or, like his boss, intoxicated, as he just stood there with a vacant look on his face while he was rubbing the window with a very dirty cloth. He must have dropped it in the dirt as we could hear the sand scratching the glass.

With an, "Excuse me a minute," Angus calmly got up, walked over to the window, opened it and punched the poor bastard out cold. Had it not been for the fact that I knew him as a man that normally treated his employees with understanding and compassion, I would have refused to have any further dealings with Angus. To his further credit I must add that he immediately went outside, helped the man back on his feet and told him to take the rest of the day off.

As an introduction to Angus, that story will have to suffice for now, but let me tell you a little about my other companions. David Herschfeld was somewhat of a pioneer in the district, which had depended on cattle ranching until David decided to hire a water diviner to look for underground water. The diviner spent days walking around the farm with his crooked little diviner stick suspended between his two index fingers. David's neighbors, who had been following the progress, or lack thereof, with great interest, soon started cracking jokes about it. "David my man, you better be careful you don't drown in all that water, or can you walk on the stuff, like that relative of yours?"

But David and his diviner persisted and in the end found a torrent of water in the second or third bore hole. He never looked back from there and neither did his neighbors who soon followed his lead, all finding plenty of underground water. Give any South African farmer rich soils and lots of water to irrigate with and he will grow an abundance of crops. David and his neighbors turned their backs to subsistence cattle farming and started making serious money growing vegetables and potatoes.

Frans Van der Merwe had spent several years in the SAAF. While there, he must have been somewhat of a hell raiser, as he was finally discharged for taking his girlfriend on an unauthorized joyride in a jet fighter. It had not altogether been a disaster for Frans as she then rewarded him by becoming his wife. He was a lucky man as Josi was a very smart cookie and a real sweetheart.

On a Friday, late in the afternoon, the four of us set out on our 250 mile flight to Johannesburg. Immediately things started going wrong. Less than half an hour into our flight, our two pilots noticed that the fuel gauge was indicating an almost empty tank. As it was full on take-off, either the gauge was faulty, or we had a serious fuel leak and might soon have a dry tank. Fortunately, many farmers had landing strips on their farms and Frans landed us safely on the first one we spotted. On the ground we determined that there was no leak and the tank full. We were air borne again in a matter of minutes.

I expressed the hope that the faulty gauge was an isolated defect and not a symptom of a more general electrical problem. For that I was loudly denounced as a pessimist and spoilsport.

The remainder of the flight to the Jan Smuts International Airport near Johannesburg was uneventful. Frans was well-known among the traffic controllers there, and they let us land between two commercial flights that arrived only minutes apart, something they would not have allowed of a less experienced pilot. In spite of all that experience, this maneuver seemed rather hairy to me. Not wanting to be accused of being a spoilsport again, I held my peace. According to Angus, there had been enough time to land a small squadron of Cessnas.

The South African cricketers lost the series, but we had a good time and did our fair share of consuming beer on the stands. So much so that on our drive back to the hotel after the first day of cricket in very congested, slow moving traffic, David decided he needed to take an urgent leak. At the time we were on a stretch of urban highway with no exit in sight and bumper to bumper cars moving at five miles per hour. I stopped the car and David calmly proceeded to take his leak along the side of the road accompanied by a concert of catcalls and horns blown in protest, or perhaps in support.

During the next day of cricket, Angus managed to get into a fight with an Englishman, who kept making snide remarks about South Africans that did not know how to play this game and that nothing better was to be expected, as cricket was a gentleman's game.

An exchange of insults was followed by Angus attempting to escort the Limey out of the stadium. Unsuccessfully I might add, as the security guys soon intervened and then escorted all of us out of the stadium, which suited me fine, as by that time I had seen enough cricket to last me for the rest of my life.

By now it was three in the afternoon and it was decided to fly home that same day. Frans assured us that there was plenty of time and even if we arrived after dark, he had no problem with that. We would simply radio ahead to Josi, who could park a car with lights on at the beginning of the landing strip on his farm. He had done it many times! When we had finally picked up our stuff at the hotel and arrived at the airport, there was only one hour to sundown and it would be pitch black by the time we were to arrive. My feeble protestations and suggestion that we might leave in the morning were firmly overruled. I did not have too many options. I was either going to have to take my chances with these cowboys or find my way back by train and bus as no airline flew to our neck of the woods.

Less than an hour after takeoff the cabin lights went off and not very much later the panel of gauges and dials lost its

129

illumination. We were on a compass course, but as it was getting dark rapidly, the compass would soon no longer be readable. We were royally screwed. I should have taken the train after all! My misgivings about the electrical systems of this little plane were being substantiated in a dramatic manner. The only thing that still seemed to function was the engine. The navigation lights had also quit.

Our pilots deliberated for a little and decided to find a landing spot while there was still a little daylight left. Frans reassured us with the info that he knew of a large sugar plantation, and they had a first class landing strip where we would touch down. Radio contact was attempted, but also that part of our system failed. As the light was fading rapidly I was getting more than a little concerned and guardedly suggested that we should perhaps just put it down on a country road while we could more or less see where we were going. Frans agreed, and while starting his descent he pulled the lever that was supposed to release the landing gear.

Well you guessed it. That essential bit of equipment also depended on electricity, a commodity of which we appeared to have none.

"Power failures on the ground are a nuisance, but you can always make do with candles," observed Angus.

"Alright guys, it is going to be a belly landing, tighten your seatbelts," instructed Frans. "I am going to put it down in the sugarcane as that will provide some measure of cushioning. Here we go. Sorry boys, but don't worry, I have done this before."

I don't know what prevented me from pissing my pants, but some way or other I just sat there and took careful note of the events that followed. Frans told David, his co-pilot, to shove his seat back as far as it could go and protect his face with his hands and to make sure not to touch any of the controls. He instructed the two of us on the rear seat to lean forward and protect our faces in the same way.

Cool as a cucumber he then reduced speed to just above stalling, cut the engine and while bringing the nose slightly up slid the little plane into the sugarcane. Initially there was just a lot of noise caused by the young cane stalks slapping the plane, but when we really started to hit the deck the noise became deafening while we were banged around mercilessly. All I could think of at the time was, *you should have taken the train you fool!* There was none of that, "seeing your entire life go by in a flash."

After what seemed to be a very long time, all noise and movement ceased. We had come to a complete stop and miraculously the plane was upright.

Frans had us out of there in seconds and apart from a cut over David's eye none of us were any the worse for wear.

Angus just wondered, "Where the hell are we going to get a beer now!"

David seemed to have suddenly found religion and said a little prayer in Hebrew, "Baruch Hashem," which, freely translated means, "Thank the Lord." For once, we all shared this sentiment.

Frans assured us, "Well, that was a piece of cake. I told you I had done this before!"

For the first time on this trip I was sort of dumbstruck, but promised myself never to see another cricket match and to stay out of planes that did not at least have two big jet engines and a nice reassuring airline logo, such as KLM, DELTA, SAA or the like. Come to think of it, I have to this day, remained true to fifty percent of that resolve.

I never went to see another cricket match.

Chapter 17

THE DALMATIAN THAT WASN'T

During my days in South Africa, large parts of the country were still relatively remote and isolated. As roads were often not much more than rough dirt tracks that would be rendered practically impassable by some heavy showers, few outsiders were motivated to visit these places. Some of the small towns in these parts harbored an array of very unusual characters. Apart from isolation, there was apartheid and last but not least the political strife and outright hate between the Afrikaner and the English-speaking inhabitants. All these things shaped the society and its members. The anecdotes I am to relate were not directly shaped by any of these factors, but it can also be argued that the environment always influences everything that happens between people. I suspect that the very hot weather of the Northern Transvaal also had something to do with it. One little town, where my work took me on a regular basis, harbored more than its fair share of very strange characters.

For instance, there were two small banks in this country town, practically next door to each other. They were

133

owned by the Lewis brothers. Frank and Marius were twins and disliked each other with unimaginable depth of feeling. I never discovered what caused all this hate and suspect they barely knew its origins themselves.

Originally, there had been one Lewis Bank that the boys inherited from their father. The legend goes that they fought each other relentlessly until Marius took his brother to court with a claim for half of the business. In the end some sort of agreement was arrived at. With the proceeds, Marius bought a nearby lot and built his own Lewis Bank. The ensuing competition was fierce to the huge benefit of the locals. In the end both Lewis Banks went belly-up and the remnants were picked up by the big boys in Johannesburg. So much for brotherly love.

And then there was Clifford Lloyd. Cliff was a young bachelor who lived and worked with his parents on a nearby farm. His father was a good customer of mine and that is how I met Cliff for the first time. He was wild, funny and totally irresponsible, and after putting a young girl in the family way, had to get married to her. I remember him telling me, "Hey man, I put her 'up the pole' and now her father is threatening to shoot me if I don't marry her."

That his career as a rampaging bachelor came to a sudden and predictable end was no surprise to anyone who had ever partied with him. One of his frequent pronouncements had been that the "legal age" for sexual activity was determined by the weight and/or the age of the girl in question. "Sixteen years old or 100 pounds, whichever comes first." Apparently, he had not just been joking as the girl he ended up marrying—shotgun style—gave birth to his son before she was quite sixteen years old. She did however exceed the weight criteria he had set himself, by a large margin.

Cliff was not a bad husband and father—if measured against the local standards—but an extremely uncooperative son-in-law. He soon developed an intensive dislike for his wife's meddling mother, and I have to admit she was not what you might refer to as a sweet old lady. I have no doubt that her actions were well intended to benefit her daughter and grandson, but dictating when Clifford was allowed to sleep with his wife was obviously going well beyond her motherly duties. She also had her excessive weight to her disadvantage and Clifford used to refer to her openly as, "That pig—she looks like and weighs about the same as the sow we will be slaughtering soon."

It was about half a year after the birth of his son that I encountered him on a bright Saturday morning, pushing a wheelbarrow covered with sackcloth through the village. This was shortly before Christmas and the town was teeming with the farmers from the surrounding area doing their banking and shopping. Clifford was pushing his wheelbarrow with a big smile on his mug and whenever he was asked what he was transporting, he obligingly lifted the cloth to display the head of the sow that had just been butchered and then explained; "I'm just taking my mother in law for a walk and a Merry Christmas to you."

So much for married bliss.

Well, as I said that little town had more than its fair share of crazies and this last example will probably suffice to fully make my point.

135

Blackie Cronje, who was as white as a lily, lived on his own on the outskirts of the village with his dog Missy and, as was widely rumored, with his maid. Like all maids in nineteen-sixties South Africa, she was black. And she was also reported to be very attractive. Living with your maid, if the maid was black and you were white, was very illegal and socially not acceptable. As a result of this his neighbors shunned him and the police had once raided his place. They had however not been able to bring concrete proof of unlawful intimacy.

Blackie did not work and he did not need to because he had inherited a lot of money from his father, who had been a prominent engineer and mining prospector for the gold mines. He spent his days loafing around the house and yard and could often be found on his porch drinking beer and smoking cigars.

His isolation from his fellow white fellow citizens was not primarily the result of his interracial activity. Nobody would of course openly admit it, but many of the old-timers in those parts had sampled the erotic wares *offered* by the local women. And what was not offered could always be taken, as most treated their black workers as if they owned them.

Blackie would sit on his porch with a rifle handy, ready to shoot any dog that happened to stray into his yard. Blackie's dog Missy, a female seemingly in perpetual heat, attracted many of the males in the neighborhood and quite a number had thus met their maker.

No complaints to the police would help the poor owners of these dogs because according to local law, a person had the right to shoot marauding dogs that strayed on his land. This was the main reason Blackie had few friends among his neighbors. They were looking for revenge and had for some time been hatching a plan. They came up with a brilliant, but rather cruel strategy.

During one of Blackie's weekly trips to the bank and hardware store, presumably to replenish on ammo, they kidnapped Missy with the intention to release her again when the time was right.

Missy was a rather ugly, white mongrel with long hair. After capturing her they shaved her and then polka dotted her with black paint. She now looked more or less like the Dalmatian of one of Blackie's neighbors. Then they waited until dusk and made sure that Blackie was in position on the porch with the gun at his side. He sat there, at intervals calling and whistling for his Missy. They released her and like the good dog she was, she made a beeline for home where Blackie shot her dead before she was halfway across the yard.

Herman Thorbecke

Chapter 18

APARTHEID AT ITS WORST

One of my friends at college, Fred Van Houten, also came to South Africa. He arrived there after a stint in Nyasaland, now Malawi, where he had worked as a supervisor on one of the coffee plantations. I don't know what happened that made him leave there and come south—perhaps a world-wide glut in coffee—but it soon proved to be a bad mistake.

Fred, while still in college, married the daughter of one of our professors. Professor Kerkdijk taught us the elements of organic chemistry and was of Javanese (Indonesian) origins. And just so you may see the connection, Indonesia, that fabulous archipelago of thousands of islands, became an independent nation during 1949 when the Dutch, after 350 years of colonization recognized its independence. When that happened many Indonesians with strong ties to Holland opted to come to the "mother country." Professor Kerkdijk, who was married to a Dutch woman probably did not have too many choices. He came to Holland and there his daughter married Fred.

Marieke was extremely beautiful and could easily pass as someone born and bred in the Netherlands. Her complexion was fair, her eyes a lively black and her hair a curly, reddish brown. Only the old hands at race discrimination would have recognized the telltale signs of Oriental parentage. She was also smart and with her degree in political sciences from the University of Amsterdam, she could have had a brilliant carrier in the diplomatic service. Marieke must have loved Fred a whole lot to have followed him to Nyasaland and later to South Africa.

Her racial background during their move to Nyasaland, then under British rule, had in no way been an obstacle. The British, to their credit, only practiced racial segregation among the upper classes. However, South Africa was an entirely different matter. The Lord only knows what made them decide to come to the most race segregated country in the world. Believe me, the USA during the sixties with its Jim Crow laws in the South came only a close second. The fact that he managed to obtain South African entry visas for his family must be attributed to some error made by an embassy staff member in Blantyre. Normally, the SA Government only admitted immigrants of pure Caucasian descent.

We had over the years exchanged some correspondence. He had written to me about his plans to come to the Transvaal and I had tried to warn him that Marieke's family background might prevent him from obtaining entry visas. Some six months later I received an invitation to come and visit them at their new home in the Transvaal. They had moved to a large farm in the Lowveld, some 125 miles south from where we lived. He had been appointed managing director of a large citrus estate in the Crocodile River Valley. I knew the place well as I had lived in that same area some years earlier. He had really hit the big times as that particular farm was probably the largest and most advanced citrus producer in the country. On the very first opportunity I packed my family in the car to go and visit Fred and Marieke for a long weekend.

We had not seen each other since we left college. It was a joyful reunion that was amply celebrated with good beer and the Dutch national drink, Genever. For the uninitiated, Genever is a type of gin made from corn and/or potatoes, comes in stone jars and is certain to cause much pleasure, followed by ample pain and discomfort. That part is practically guaranteed.

As we arrived in the evening after the children's bedtime, our two complete families only got together the next day at breakfast. I knew from our correspondence that they had two kids, but had never seen them. Neely was about eleven, blond and looked like her dad. Arend was a beautiful little boy of five and strongly resembled his grandpa Kerkdijk. The kid had the complexion, hair and facial features of a typical Javanese boy, a boy that would most likely never be admitted to the local schools unless it was one designated for non-European children.

My son Bert, an old hand at racial matters after eight years in that country, took me aside later during the day and asked me, "Did Uncle Fred and Aunt Marieke adopt Arend and where is he going to go to school?"

I improvised, "No, he is their son. He is just a little darker in color than most Dutch people."

I did not offer a reply to the second part of his question.

141

All in all we had a very enjoyable visit. Fred proudly showed us around the estate, a multi-million dollar operation that was well known for exporting large quantities of its fruit to Great Britain and Europe and operated its own juicing facility.

That evening Fred and Marieke had invited a number of the management staff to a lively party and cookout that was held at the estate guesthouse, a fancy facility, serviced by a swarm of Africans and equipped with Tiki bar, a swimming pool and an enormous out-side grill. As it was to be a family affair, most had brought their kids, who were soon all over the pool, screeching and screaming like only kids will. It was a good time for all with only one sour note, and that came from one of the little girls that loudly complained, while pointing at Arend, that she would not get into the pool as long as the colored kid was in there. Indoctrinated as she was by her environment, she did not know any better. Her parents did and had the good sense to leave early, but the damage had been done. Soon, some of the other children also got out of the water and it wasn't long until only Fred's and our kids and those of a German employee were still in the water. Our explanation was that European kids were really crazy about swimming. The embarrassment was extreme. Fred, in order to hold up appearances, tried to ignore the whole thing, but poor Marieke was beside herself and disappeared inside the house to remain there for the rest of the evening. Apartheid had raised its ugly head again.

Later that night after the other guests had left, Marieke confided that she had the feeling that some of the white women among the estate employees shunned her company. Initially she had attributed all this to her own heightened awareness of race, but on several occasions, she had noticed that conversation had abruptly halted on her approach. Moreover, if looks had been able to kill, her little Arend would have been dead long ago.

"What is it with these people? I know they are racists, but I was used to that, as even in Holland I was often subjected to that type of treatment. But here it is extreme. I feel they really hate us and I am not sure I will be able to survive in this environment. What are we going to do when Arend has to go to school? I suppose I have no other choice than to teach him at home."

I attempted to ease her distress and said, "You are probably overreacting a little. It's very upsetting, but I'm sure that once they have had time to get used to you, things will get better. Keep in mind that many of these people are angry that an "Uitlander" (foreigner) was appointed to be the boss. You can be sure most of these women believe that their husbands should have been picked for the job. Jealousy plus a little racism and you end up with a nasty emotional cocktail. I'm sure it will fade over time."

She just said, "I so hope you are right, but I have my doubts."

She was right of course. After our short visit there, a few months went by before they came and spent a mini-vacation with us, during which we invited some of our friends for a party. To make sure that Marieke and Arend would not be subjected to the nastiness of racial prejudice, we only invited people we could rely on to be totally indifferent to the color of anyone's skin. Because of that, it was not a very big party, but we all had a good time.

Marieke confided to my wife that she saw no future for her and the children in South Africa. She was trying to convince Fred to resign from his job and look for greener and less racial pastures somewhere else. Trouble was that he had signed a three-year contract. Also, he did not seem to think the whole affair was that much of a problem, and according to my wife that was typical of men and their egocentric attitudes. I am afraid she based her views in this respect entirely on her experience with her own man. Mea culpa!

Some months later Fred called to let us know that Marieke had returned to Holland with the children. During a visit there a month earlier she applied for a job in the Dutch diplomatic service and had been offered a good position. The plan was for him to stay in South Africa for the remainder of his contract after which he would reevaluate his options.

He told me, "I will never get another chance like this, particularly if I don't complete my contract. I am making a lot of money and if the crop is going to be as good as it was last year, I stand to pick up a bonus that's bigger than my annual salary. Marieke will wait for me and besides, I can go and see the family on short visits every year."

I told him, "Fred, you dumb son-of-a-bitch, if you are not careful you will lose your family. Legally you are in your full rights if you claim that the racial atmosphere over here is intolerable and therefore ground for breach of contract. You can't even send your own kid to school unless you send him to the mission school with the other blacks."

I should not have said that. He told me to fuck off and mind my own business. From that day, we did not hear from Fred for a very long time. Marieke stayed in touch and wrote regularly telling us she was worried about Fred. At the termination of his contract, he had apparently signed a new one for one year and told her he would repatriate after that. I called him a couple of times. We made polite conversation, but the friendly familiarity was gone.

A couple months after my last call, I had to attend a company conference in Nelspruit only a few miles from his place. One of the evenings, just after dinner, I decided to take a chance and drove out to his home. On parking the car in front of his bungalow, I saw one of the servants leaving in a hurry through one of the side doors, but thought nothing of it at the time. Fred came out on the veranda, seemed somewhat flustered and preoccupied, but received me with an invitation to sit down while he went in to get us some beers. That in itself was somewhat unusual. At the time of my previous visit, there had been an array of African women doing the serving. I presumed that now, while he was on his own, he sort of took care of himself. The conversation came sparingly. When I asked him for news from his family he curtly answered, "Things are fine. You don't have to worry about her. She found herself this fancy job and has already been promoted. There even is talk about her being posted at the Dutch embassy in Djakarta, Indonesia."

I said, "Wow. That is fantastic. You could join her there, couldn't you?"

"Yah, right, and be her houseboy?"

From there the conversation went downhill even further and I soon got the message that my visit really wasn't welcome at all. I finished my beer and took my leave, realizing that our friendship had sort of reached rock bottom. I expressed my hope that things would work out for them and got in the car. On driving away from the house, I saw the same woman I had seen leaving on my arrival, now entering the house again. What was going on there?

Another six months went by before we heard from Fred again. He sounded very agitated and asked if he could come and stay for a couple of days. He just said that he had terminated his contract and that he was on his way home. The call came at five in the afternoon. My wife assured him that he was welcome and he had arrived at the house soon after. I wasn't home at that time, but when I drove up, about an hour later, Fred was already installed on our veranda with a cold beer in his hand. Apparently, he had called from a small motel nearby and he now told us he was driving north to Salisbury, Southern Rhodesia, where he would catch a plane to Amsterdam. That seemed a little strange as the shorter and quicker way would have been to drive to Johannesburg and fly out of there. However no more was said about that and after a couple more beers he started to relax a little. My wife and kids had gone to sleep and the two of us were still working on the beers when he broke down and started to reveal what was really going on.

"I'm in deep shit man. I think the police are looking for me and I have to get across the border to Rhodesia. Will you help me please? You can smuggle me over the border if I hide in the trunk of the car."

The entire story then came in spurts. He had felt lonely, and while he had been in bed with a bad case of dysentery, Sara, his housemaid, had taken care of him and one night had offered to stay in the room with him. Well one thing had led to another and soon she was sharing his bed on a regular basis. Sara was young, smart and very pretty. In a way he had become totally attached to her. She was always there for him, truly devoted and had given him better sex than he had ever experienced. I did not tell him so, but as I had some experience, I could well believe that. The trouble started when Sara's brother, who worked on the farm as a laborer, had become suspicious and had been seen snooping around.

Sara had warned Fred that he might cause trouble, and as a precaution, Fred told her to sleep outside the house for the time being. It wasn't much later that the man had showed up one late afternoon after work. He said, "Baas, me Simon. You like my sister? If you like her you can have her. What you pay for my sister?"

He had told him, "Fuck off, I don't want your sister. You show up here again and you will lose your job."

"Baas, my job is to take care of my sister and you will pay. I will never have to work again."

Fred had seen red, entered the house and came out with his shotgun, with which he had threatened the man.

Marieke, not Fred, was the trained diplomat. Retreating cautiously, Simon then had told him, "My sister is having your baby and I will ask Polisi what to do."

He had then left in a hurry, leaving Fred wishing he had never set foot in South Africa. That same evening Sara had shown up with a swollen eye from being punched by Simon and had confirmed that she was expecting,

"Baas is not to worry. I can make baby go away, but very expensive."

He had paid her the paltry sum she had demanded and

had not seen her or the brother again for several weeks, until Simon had again showed up, just hanging around the house. A few days later, a golfing friend of Fred's, an assistant prosecutor, had called and asked if he could come over for a chat. The man, a good friend apparently, told him that Simon had reported the affair to the police and that there were rumors that an investigation into the matter might follow. Although his office had strongly recommended dropping the whole thing, he suggested that Fred should speak to a lawyer and be prepared just in case something would come of it. According to Fred the man had practically insinuated that he get out while he could.

That had been a few days ago. Fred had stayed on the job, but not being able to sleep, he had turned into a total wreck from worry. What was he to do? Wait it out, hoping that it would all blow over, or get out of the country before the police came to arrest him? He decided to leave and had told his assistant that he needed to go to Cape Town for a couple of days on personal business. He had his secretary book him a flight from Johannesburg to the city of the Table Mountain. Before he left he cashed out most of his bank account and in order not to cause suspicion had left a few thousand rand. He had told the bank manager he was going to make a cash offer on a farm on the Komati River. He then got into his personal car, a brand-new Peugeot 404, and drove north with the plan to drive across the border to Salisbury. On the way he started getting a little paranoid and wondered, what if? What if they were already looking for him and closed the border? That's how he ended up at our place.

"Herman, you probably think I am crazy and I admit

148

that nothing might come of the whole thing, but I don't want to run the risk of ending up in one of their prisons. I would rather kill myself. Please get me over the border."

I thought about this for a while and not knowing how far this thing had gone, arrived at the conclusion that going to Rhodesia would not be safe either. That government was just as racist and had all sorts of agreements with the South Africans, which meant that even if he managed to get across the border, they would likely be looking out for him at the airports.

I said, "Fred if you want to be really safe, you need to go to Mozambique and fly out of Lorenzo Marques. The Portuguese do not practice official segregation and have few agreements with this country. Once through the SA border post you are home free. For a fleeting moment I thought perhaps I am in the grip of the same paranoia that has him in its spell.

Fred immediately agreed. "You are absolutely right. Why did I not think of that? Will you get me across? When can we leave?"

"Hold it, Fred. I have a family to consider and am not sure I want to risk getting caught at the border, illegally transporting a fugitive. We'd both end up in jail and if they put us in the same cell, we're likely to end up killing each other," I joked.

I was friendly with a farmer that owned land on the border of Mozambique and was wondering if we could get Fred and his Peugeot across in the course of a little Safari on that farm. Some years ago, on one of our hunting trips we had wandered into Portuguese territory and actually ended up in a little town on the other side of the border, drinking wine in the local bodega. The local policeman had asked no questions and actually joined us for a glass or two.

After I told Fred this little story, he again asked, "When can we leave?"

"I know you really want to go home to Marieke and the children, but I need to talk to this farmer first and find out if it's all right with him."

On that note we agreed to sleep on it and continue our plans in the morning.

The next day I called my farmer friend and told him a story about a friend of mine that wanted to study a certain type of vegetation common to the area where his farm was located. Would he mind if we spent a day or two looking around on his farm? He had no problem with that, as long as we did not need him to accompany us as he was going away on vacation for a couple of weeks. It could not have been better. We would have the free run of his farm. Fred could slip over the border with his Peugeot and I would drive home in my four-wheel drive Landrover that would come in handy for towing Fred's car in the event it would get bogged down in the sand.

A couple days later we drove south, circumvented the Nelspruit area, where Fred might be recognized, and drove to my friend's farm just south of Komatipoort. Once there I spoke to the foreman and asked him if he could lend me a good tracker that knew the area well. He recommended Jacob, who was quite happy to come for the ride, particularly as I offered him a couple of rand for getting Fred across the border. He only expressed one reservation, "Baas, I don want go into zambiki country. Polisi very bad there. They beat me real bad last year."

I told him, "Not to worry Jacob. You just bring us to the border, and then we go back."

Our trip to the border was not uneventful. The Peugeot did not get stuck, but we almost got ourselves killed. While driving through the bush in the border area, and after just having driven through some really nasty acacia bush, we were suddenly confronted with a couple of armed blacks that must have been on a poaching trip. They were retreating on foot and at a distance of some hundred yards, when I first noticed them. They must have heard us coming and had been trying to get away, unseen. When we emerged from the dense bush, they fired a couple of shots that fortunately went wide. As a precaution I had taken a pump action shotgun and let them have a couple loads of game shot. I am sure I did not hurt anything other than their feelings, but it sure helped to make up their minds to leave in a hurry.

From there on we cautiously moved forward until we came to a drivable bush track. By that time Jacob was more than a little agitated and told me he wanted his money so he could go home. I told him if he hung around a little longer I would drive him back, but he would have none of that and said, "Baas, the Zambiki polisi no good. They will kill me if they catch me in their country."

I paid him and he assured me he had no problem walking home the ten or so miles back to the farm house. The track we had found led us to the same little village I had visited on my last trip. There we relaxed for a while with a cool cerveza and some delicious prawns, got directions to the capital, Lorenzo Marques (now Maputo), and Fred was safely on his way home.

I drove back the way we had come and a couple of miles from the homestead picked up Jacob who was happy to get a ride for the last bit of his journey and told me, "Baas, you very brave (read stupid) to go into that Zambiki country. The tzotzies could have killed us if they had waited for you behind trees. Those people real killers. We very lucky with good medicine!"

We achieved what we had set out to do, but I had taken a stupid risk and although my "medicine" had protected me again, I wondered if and when my luck would finally run out.

A week later Fred called to let me know he had arrived in Holland via Lisbon and was happily back with his family. He had left his car in the parking lot of the Polana Hotel and the key at the hotel desk with instructions to give them to me only.

He said, "The car is yours now and I don't want to hear any arguments about that. All you have to do is go there and pick it up. Thanks again for all you have done for me."

Marieke had accepted the position at the embassy in Djakarta and he was hopeful he might find some sort of job in Indonesia. He asked me to do him a final favor and find out from his friend, the assistant prosecutor, if anything had come of the "Immorality Act" case against him.

I did make that call and was told that it had been dropped. Apparently, Sara's brother had recanted his statement and Fred would have no problems in the event he wanted to return. Sara's brother must have been under some severe pressure to recant. Perhaps Fred's former employers, reluctant to lose a good manager, stepped in and had a quiet word with the local Police Chief?

I sold the Peugeot and sent Fred the proceeds.

Ndebele woman in her finery as one might find her in
The Transvaal Lowveld during the sixties

Herman Thorbecke

Chapter 19

IRISH AND EMERALD GREEN

The first time I met Kevin Doyle he was in the bar of the Tzaneen Hotel celebrating his birthday and merrily inebriated. In those years that was the only hotel in town and the only bar within miles. My friend, Michael van Meter, introduced me to him.

"Hey there, Kevin, meet Herman Thorbecke. We have come to help you celebrate whatever it is you are celebrating today."

Kevin, who was short, stocky and judging from his brogue, Irish, grabbed my hand and looking up at me while trying to rip my arm from its socket said, "Mr. Tallbugger it's a pleasure to meet you. Have a drink. It's my birthday and I am celebrating indeed." His interpretation of my name was rewarded with hilarity and I am afraid it sort of stuck for some time. At 6'3" and compared to his scant 5'6", I suppose I was tall, if not a bugger.

The bar at the Tzaneen Hotel was a grand affair. Its horseshoe shape could easily accommodate some fifty to sixty customers. On most days of the week, farmers and trades people from the area frequented the place. On Fridays it was always packed with a noisy and often rowdy crowd. Fistfights were common, the details of which could be read about in the local rag, as the editor of the Tzaneen Weekly was a regular customer himself.

As I was relatively new to the area, Michael filled me in on who-was-who and who-did-what. Among other tidbits of information was that Kevin Doyle had a small cattle farm in the area and was known as a bit of a "prospector." It appears that the police had repeatedly suspected and questioned him about his activities relevant to the illegal trade in emeralds. Although they had never been able to pin anything on Kevin, everybody seemed to know that he was involved. What may have given him away was the fact that while his farming operation was relatively minor, he practiced a rather opulent lifestyle, which involved a private plane and very expensive cars.

Emeralds formed a sideline product at the open pit Phalaborwa mine, a big commercial operation not far from Tzaneen. A large number of different minerals were mined there, and although emeralds only played a minor role in the larger scope of things, these precious stones were jealously guarded and all attempts at clandestine harvesting or dealing were vigorously suppressed. The company had its own private police force and it was rumored that its chief had for years been trying to pin something on Kevin.

South Africa's Wealth: People, Gold and Diamonds

He had come very close once, when some years earlier, during a routine search, a large rough emerald had been found on Kevin's girlfriend of the moment. Fortunately, for Kevin, the girl, very pretty and far from stupid, had explained the gemstone's presence in her pocket by saying she had found it on the road and had taken it for some pretty green stone without any value. She had stuck to her original tale, even under some severe pressure and threats of prosecution for prostitution, for which many knew, there might have been some cause. It was rumored that Kevin had rewarded her with an even bigger stone. The one that had been confiscated was said to be valued at ten thousand Rand. Probably an overstatement since Kevin, although generous, did not simply give his money away without good cause. Good cause being a debatable notion.

During the several years since my first encounter with Kevin, we met repeatedly and became, if not close friends, good acquaintances. Sometimes we met by chance at the Tzaneen Hotel bar and later also socially at the homes of mutual friends. Although I am rather proud of what is a famous and well-known name in the Netherlands, I was never much offended by his way of referring to me as "Tall Bugger." To his credit I must mention that after some time, when the joke had worn thin, he started calling me by my first name. Not everyone had taken the hint, and on a couple of occasions I had to remind people forcefully that my name was Thorbecke.

We had Kevin over for dinner once and on several occasions we were over at his place. One of them remains in memory as a grand and rather rowdy event that featured live music and belly dancers, both black and white. He also served one of the biggest cookouts I had ever witnessed. Meat of all possible variations, from undercooked to "alive" was being served to a very receptive gathering in which all levels of the Tzaneen society were well represented. I clearly recollect that the local prosecutor and his wife appeared to have a great time, while a judge from nearby Petersburg, sans wife, seemed to be very interested in one of the live offerings.

Michael van Meter, filling me in on the exploits of Kevin told me that he had arrived in the Lowveld some ten years ago from the Kimberley area. Most of you have heard of the famous Big Hole diamond mine in Kimberley, owned by the De Beers Company and located in the Northern Cape Province of South Africa. While the Big Hole mine was abandoned long before Kevin's residency there, diamonds were still mined in the region. The story went that Kevin had made a small fortune acquiring and selling illegally obtained stones in Kimberley. I was told that he had only moved to "greener" pastures—Phalaborwa—after the police, never having caught him red-handed, had started covering all his moves to the extent that making an "honest" living had become impossible for him.

The final straw for the Kimberley Police Chief had come when Kevin again evaded arrest after a very carefully set trap had snapped shut without Kevin in it. The police trap involved a lucrative deal in contraband diamonds that were being offered by one of the employees of the company. The plan was kept secret, and even the fellow that was to hand over the stones in exchange for cash did not know it was a trap. Kevin had shown interest in the deal, but from the beginning had been suspicious. His overly mistrustful character had kept him out of trouble for years and he was not about to get careless.

It had all been planned in detail and it was agreed that the exchange would take place on top of a large bridge over the Orange River. The rendezvous was to happen at two in the morning on Monday. A time of the day and week when there was no traffic at all. In their eagerness to catch the big fish at last, the police overlooked the fact that Kevin had made it a condition to meet on top of the bridge at that odd time. Kevin had also instructed the "seller" to arrive on foot and that he would approach from the south side of the bridge by car.

The police chief agreed to the conditions and on the night the deal was to transpire had a small contingent of his men strategically positioned on the north side of the bridge. They were ready to arrest Kevin as soon as he came down the bridge on his way home, which they well knew was less than a mile from the north side of the bridge. Shortly before two in the morning, the headlights of a car were seen coming up the bridge. They stayed on for a while, just long enough to illuminate the scene while the exchange was made, the money counted and the wares inspected. They were then turned off and for some time nothing seemed to happen. After a while the seller came walking down the bridge where he was received with open arms by the police. There was however no sign of Kevin.

It was then that the Police Chief realized he had been misled again. Apparently Kevin had reversed up his side of the bridge in a pickup truck, on the back of which he had mounted a set of powerful headlights. After the deal had been completed he simply freewheeled the vehicle noiselessly down the slope of the bridge, the same way he had come. Once all the way down he started the car and drove non-stop over the border into the Orange Free State. From there he went to Johannesburg, where he sold the stones at a fat profit. When the police came to inspect his house, they found its new owner. Kevin had sold it for cash on the day before. A couple of weeks later he had shown up in Tzaneen where he had invested his "savings" into a nice little farm that happened to border on the Phalaborwa mine property.

One of my last encounters with Kevin Doyle took place a few months before I left South Africa to return to Europe. I had met a customer for dinner at the Tzaneen Hotel and while we were on our way to the bar for an after-dinner drink, Kevin, who seemed to be in rather a hurry, bumped heavily into me. He then grabbed me, took me in a bear hug and told me, "I am so glad to see you Herman. Don't be a stranger.

Come see me sometime soon and bring the family. Make sure now as otherwise I will come and get you."

He slapped me on the back and vanished down the corridor. My customer and I looked at each other in amazement. We both knew Kevin for his eccentric behavior, but this performance had been very much out of character. First, he wasn't much into hugging guys and second, although he knew my customer well he had totally ignored him. We enjoyed our excellent, twenty-year-old KWV brandies and I had forgotten the entire episode by the time I came home.

It was July and mid-winter. In that part of the country, it means that the nights are refreshingly cool or sometimes even cold. After parking the car in my driveway, I decided to stroll around the moonlit garden a little. Perhaps the cold air would help to clear the alcoholic fog from my brain. I pulled up the collar of the tweed wool jacket I was wearing and stuck my hands into the side pockets. Nice and warm. However, what was this thing in my pocket? I fished it out and examined it by the bright light of the moon. I was holding a small, bulging leather pouch and I immediately guessed what it contained.

I hurried to go inside, making sure to be quiet so as not to wake my wife and kids. In my office, after closing the shades, I released the pull string of the little bag and dumped its contents onto my desk. Out spilled a nice handful of pretty, green rocks. Little rocks. Big emeralds. A small fortune in emeralds. Kevin must have shoved them into my pocket at the time of his out-of-character hug. Eventually one always finds an explanation for odd behavior. After examining the stones for a while and wondering what the value might be, I placed them securely into the safe and went to bed. Tomorrow would be another day.

In the morning I made up my mind to let some days go by before getting in touch with Kevin. He must have suspected that the police were on to him when, on the spur of the moment, he had freed himself of the incriminating evidence. I suppose I should have been angry with him for exposing and involving me in this dangerous business. Some way or other I did not really mind though. Nobody would suspect me and I knew that if I played it right, he would probably reward me well. Hey, nothing wrong with picking up a little severance pay before going back to Europe.

And sure enough, after about a fortnight, Kevin called to invite me and the family for a "braai" (cook-out) on his farm. I accepted his "kind" invitation and asked if we could bring anything.

"Most certainly and also bring your swimsuits. I am inviting all my friends with kids to break in my new swimming pool. We will drink some good wine while the kids have fun in the pool. Oh, and by the way, plan to stay the night. I hear you are getting ready to go back to Europe and I want to have a last opportunity to enjoy your company, if you know what I mean."

He managed to make this invitation sound like a summons. He did not offer me a choice. The message was clear. Better be there, or suffer the consequences. That, at least, was the way it sounded to me.

My wife, our three kids and I showed up for the party on time and they all had a lot of fun. Kevin's new pool was magnificent and although everybody enjoyed themselves tremendously, I could not relax. I was nervous as hell and wondered when might be the right moment to hand over the rocks that were making a rather big bulge in my pants pocket—somewhat like an uncontrollable and embarrassing hard-on. I did not dare take it out of my pocket. To camouflage it I walked around with a towel that I nonchalantly held in front of me, ostensibly to have it ready for the kids if they ever emerged from the pool, which they only did to dive in again immediately.

I had not mentioned the contraband to Fredy—no point in worrying her with that sort of stuff. Kevin was his usual affable self and paid special attention to her and my kids. It all had an eerie and unnerving atmosphere for me. The man was a gangster and who knew what he would do next? He did nothing other than to say, "Hey Herman, relax man. Your kids will be fine in the pool. Come and sit down. Have a glass of beer and take it easy. Tonight, when all the others have gone, we will sit down and talk about your return to Europe."

The evening came, the kids had gone off to sleep, and after a while, Fredy also bade us goodnight, reminding us not to drink too much of that good brandy. As soon as she had left the room, I pulled the pouch from my pocket and with great relief handed it to him. He nonchalantly shook its contents out on the coffee table. Then he carefully selected the biggest of the stones, shoved it across to my side of the table and said, "Herman, I want to apologize for involving you in this thing, but the cops had set a trap for me again. They were waiting outside the hotel to search and arrest me. When I bumped into you I was frantic. There was no way I could dispose of them without being detected and loosing this small fortune in stones. I knew I could depend on you and slipped them into your pocket. I want you to keep that one. Take it to Switzerland and sell it to this jeweler in Zurich."

He then handed me a slip of paper with a name and telephone number on it and said, "Call the guy and tell him you are a friend of mine. That way he will give you a fair deal. If I'm not mistaken it should be worth about ten-thousand Swiss Francs."

Well, he was wrong. The Swiss jeweler offered me twelve and a halve thousand. It was 1969 and I bought a nice new car with my "severance pay."

Chapter 20

MAGDALENA OF THE ZOUTPANSBERG

When people get married at eighteen years of age, they deprive themselves of experiences, they then are likely to seek at a later stage of their lives. Although we stayed together for sixteen years, we eventually went our own ways after our return to Europe.

During the latter years of my life in South Africa I did have an *affaire d'amour* with a young woman in the Northern Transvaal, for who I developed a deep and lasting affection. She lived on a farm near the Zoutpansberg Mountains, not far from the mighty and mysterious Limpopo River. Although I certainly did not realize it at the time, I suspect that my feelings for her were to a large degree influenced by her environment and lifestyle. The Bushveld in that part of Africa seems to give forth an exotic charm that may well have effected my judgment and the depth of my feelings for Magdalena.

The Limpopo, like the Zambezi, is one of the great rivers of southern Africa. To imagine what this region looks like, think of the documentaries you must have seen about

165

African wildlife. And then of course there was that fabulous movie, "Out of Africa," which was filmed not far from there. This part of Africa is known for its prolific wildlife, its majestic baobab trees and its endless savannahs with thickets of mopani trees and the infamous Wag'n Bietjie (Wait-a-little bush – Acasia cafra) that comes armed with fishhook-like thorns that will grab and hold you in an agonizing embrace.

Magdalena was like the country she lived in: wild, beautiful and unpredictable, with an embrace that easily matched the passion and unyielding grasp of the Wag'n Bietjie bush. Lena was a well-proportioned blonde with laughing eyes, lean and strong as the horses she loved to ride on her parents' 20,000 acre farm. That is a lot of land, enough to get lost on, and it was a good thing that we were together on our jaunts through the bush. On my own I might have been lost forever.

The Bushveld

Lena had a sixth sense. She was one with that country. Nothing that occurred or came within our range of vision during our horseback rides on the farm ever escaped her attention. While I needed all my faculties to stay on top of the horse and out of the grip of those thorny bushes, not always successfully, she happily galloped along, continuously commenting on the wildlife that presented itself to her attention.

"Look at that springbok, and did you see that puff adder? No? But you nearly stepped on him, you fool!" She had little patience for my inability to see and observe the wonderful show of nature that her country had to offer.

Like so many true South Africans of European descent, she spoke the local African language fluently. She had a good relationship with the farm workers, who seemed to respect her for her ability to ride a horse and rope a heifer. These people just barely acknowledged my existence and, when they did, the remarks they made to Lena made her laugh. I did, of course, not understand a word they said and on one occasion when I asked for a translation was simply told, "They are funny and don't be so paranoid. It is not always about you!"

Although I loved the Bushveld, I was more at home in the big city of Johannesburg. On our one and only visit there together, I had to hold her hand every time we crossed the street or she would have gotten herself knocked over by the wild animals on wheels. In a way it made me feel good. At least this was one area where I was permitted to take charge. To be truthful however, I really preferred spending time with her in her own environment. Even if in the beginning I did not match her love of nature, it grew on me over time. Later on I

167

had also learned to be more observant and started to notice things without her having to point them out to me.

"Look, Lena! Did you see that hawk?"

"Yes, of course I saw the bird, you think I'm blind? And by the way, it is not a hawk but a falcon."

"Yes I saw the bird"

Yes, she was a little hard on me, but we had wonderful times together and I loved her dearly. Our rides on the farm usually took us to the bank of a beautiful tributary of the Limpopo River, where we swam, and in the shade of a giant Baobab tree, loved each other with passion.

Unfortunately, as most good things have a way of coming to an end, so did my life with Lena. My new job with a multinational corporation called for me to go back to Europe and there was no way I could talk her into joining me there. I continued to write and even went back once to try to convince her, but to no avail. Futher-more, as she was not a writer, the only mail I received from her was a Christmas card, signed by the entire family and probably mailed by her mother.

You may well ask, why did you not return to South Africa?

The short answer is that Lena was one with her land, but so was I with my new powerful job and luxurious tenth floor office overlooking the Rhine as it flowed through the city of Basel.

All this happened some forty years ago, but it is often that my thoughts go back to Lena and the Bushveld of Africa. Good memories have a way of enriching one's life forever.

And then I had this dream, a really vivid dream. We were riding through the Mopani country again. Lena was on her favorite horse, an eighteen hands-tall, black thoroughbred. She was charging ahead and whatever I did, I could not catch up with her. I spurred on my horse and begged him to keep her in sight, but in the end she vanished in a cloud of dust. I woke up with a wrenching feeling of loss.

The memory of that dream left me no peace. I had to see her again. I am an old man now and what harm would be done by getting in touch?

A little Internet search revealed the email address of the family farm. I immediately wrote to her that I was planning a trip to South Africa and asked for permission to come and see her. I knew that the dream had been a signal and that I would hear from her this time. And I did. Almost immediately, there was a response.

Her son regretted to inform that his mother had recently passed away from injuries sustained during a horseback riding accident. As an old friend of the family, I was very welcome to come and visit.

The Zoutpansberg

Post Script

During the eleven years we lived in South Africa, we moved house nine times and lived in six different towns. Even though our unsettled and almost nomadic lifestyle in many ways lacked permanence and normalcy, my wife, Fredy, amply made up for that by always providing a safe and loving home for our children.

We all loved South Africa and in particular the Northern Transvaal, where we spent the last four years. Our move back to Europe was spurred on by a number of motivations, not the least of which was my ever-present restlessness. The worsening political climate and professional opportunities also played decisive roles.

For many years after our repatriation, we all looked back to our lives in South Africa with feelings of happiness, mingled with nostalgia. The following pictures are included to illustrate some of the many good time we enjoyed together.

Herman Thorbecke

Rudy, Martine and Bert in Tzaneen

Couple of monkeys

Bert on the Indian Ocean

Herman Thorbecke

Down we go!

High jump the old-fashioned way

Rudy on the rope swing

Bert, off the coast in Mozambique

The reservoir doubling as swimming pool

Martine piggybacking, Bert holding on

Rudy on veranda of the Annecke House

Martine walking the drum with Rudy looking on in awe

Made in the USA
Charleston, SC
29 September 2011